Hands-On Artificial Intelligence with Java for Beginners

Build intelligent apps using machine learning and deep learning with Deeplearning4j

Nisheeth Joshi

BIRMINGHAM - MUMBAI

Hands-On Artificial Intelligence with Java for Beginners

Commissioning Editor: Pavan Ramchandani
Acquisition Editor: Joshua Nadar
Content Development Editor: Eisha Dsouza
Technical Editor: Nilesh Sawakhande
Copy Editor: Safis Editing
Project Coordinator: Namrata Swetta
Proofreader: Safis Editing
Indexer: Rekha Nair
Graphics: Jisha Chirayil
Production Coordinator: Aparna Bhagat

First published: August 2018

Production reference: 1300818

Published by Packt Publishing Ltd.
Livery Place
35 Livery Street
Birmingham
B3 2PB, UK.

ISBN 978-1-78953-755-0

www.packtpub.com

`mapt.io`

Mapt is an online digital library that gives you full access to over 5,000 books and videos, as well as industry leading tools to help you plan your personal development and advance your career. For more information, please visit our website.

Why subscribe?

- Spend less time learning and more time coding with practical eBooks and Videos from over 4,000 industry professionals

- Improve your learning with Skill Plans built especially for you

- Get a free eBook or video every month

- Mapt is fully searchable

- Copy and paste, print, and bookmark content

PacktPub.com

Did you know that Packt offers eBook versions of every book published, with PDF and ePub files available? You can upgrade to the eBook version at `www.PacktPub.com` and as a print book customer, you are entitled to a discount on the eBook copy. Get in touch with us at `service@packtpub.com` for more details.

At `www.PacktPub.com`, you can also read a collection of free technical articles, sign up for a range of free newsletters, and receive exclusive discounts and offers on Packt books and eBooks.

Contributors

About the author

Nisheeth Joshi is an associate professor and a researcher at Banasthali University. He has also done a PhD in Natural Language Processing. He is an expert with the TDIL Program, Department of IT, Government of India, the premier organization overseeing language technology funding and research in India. He has several publications to his name in various journals and conferences, and also serves on the program committees and editorial boards of several conferences and journals.

Packt is searching for authors like you

If you're interested in becoming an author for Packt, please visit authors.packtpub.com and apply today. We have worked with thousands of developers and tech professionals, just like you, to help them share their insight with the global tech community. You can make a general application, apply for a specific hot topic that we are recruiting an author for, or submit your own idea.

Table of Contents

Preface

Artificial intelligence, which is becoming increasingly relevant in the modern world, where everything is driven by technology and data, is the process of automating any system or process to carry out complex tasks and functions automatically in order to achieve optimal productivity.

Hands-On Artificial Intelligence with Java for Beginners explains the basics of AI using popular Java-based libraries and frameworks to build your smart applications.

Who this book is for

Hands-On Artificial Intelligence with Java for Beginners is for Java developers who want to learn the fundamentals of artificial intelligence and extend their programming knowledge to build smarter applications.

What this book covers

Chapter 1, *Introduction to Artificial Intelligence and Java*, introduces artificial intelligence. It gives a very brief introduction to artificial intelligence, and how we can install and work with Java.

Chapter 2, *Exploring Search Algorithms*, will introduces two basic search techniques—Dijkstra's algorithm and the A* algorithm.

Chapter 3, *AI Games and Rule-Based System*, discusses game playing, how game playing works, how we can implement game playing in Java, what rule-based systems are, how we can implement a rule-based system, and how we can perform interfacing with rule-based systems in Java. We'll implement a rule-based system in Prolog and we'll perform the interfacing of Prolog with Java.

Chapter 4, *Interfacing with Weka*, discusses how to interact with Weka and how to perform interfacing with Weka, so the chapter covers how to download Weka and how to work with datasets.

Chapter 5, *Handling Attributes*, explains how to handle attributes while developing different kinds of classifiers and clusters. We'll also learn about different techniques for filtering attributes.

Chapter 6, *Supervised Learning*, shows how supervised models are trained, how we can develop a classifier, how we can perform evaluation on a classifier, and how we can make predictions on a classifier.

Chapter 7, *Semi-Supervised and Unsupervised Learning*, explains the differences between a supervised learning model and a semi-supervised learning model, and we'll implement a semi-supervised model.

To get the most out of this book

The prerequisites for this book are that you should have an understanding of AI, you should have taken a course on AI, and you should have a working knowledge of Java.

This book has the following software requirements:

- NetBeans 8.2
- Weka 3.8
- SWI-Prolog 7.2-7.6

This course has been tested on the following system configurations:

- OS: Windows 7, Windows 10, macOS, Ubuntu Linux 16.04 LTS
- Processor: Dual core 3.0 GHz
- Memory: 4 GB
- Hard disk space: 200 MB

Download the example code files

You can download the example code files for this book from your account at www.packtpub.com. If you purchased this book elsewhere, you can visit www.packtpub.com/support and register to have the files emailed directly to you.

You can download the code files by following these steps:

1. Log in or register at www.packtpub.com.
2. Select the **SUPPORT** tab.
3. Click on **Code Downloads & Errata**.
4. Enter the name of the book in the **Search** box and follow the onscreen instructions.

Once the file is downloaded, please make sure that you unzip or extract the folder using the latest version of:

- WinRAR/7-Zip for Windows
- Zipeg/iZip/UnRarX for Mac
- 7-Zip/PeaZip for Linux

The code bundle for the book is also hosted on GitHub at `https://github.com/PacktPublishing/Hands-On-Artificial-Intelligence-with-Java-for-Beginners`. In case there's an update to the code, it will be updated on the existing GitHub repository.

We also have other code bundles from our rich catalog of books and videos available at `https://github.com/PacktPublishing/`. Check them out!

Conventions used

There are a number of text conventions used throughout this book.

`CodeInText`: Indicates code words in text, database table names, folder names, filenames, file extensions, pathnames, dummy URLs, user input, and Twitter handles. Here is an example: "The filter that we will apply will be an unsupervised filter from the `unsupervised.attribute` package."

A block of code is set as follows:

```
Remove rmv = new Remove();
rmv.setOptions(op);
```

Any command-line input or output is written as follows:

```
?- grandfather(X, Y).
```

Bold: Indicates a new term, an important word, or words that you see onscreen. For example, words in menus or dialog boxes appear in the text like this. Here is an example: "Go to **Libraries | Add JAR/Folder** and provide the location of the `junit.jar` file."

Warnings or important notes appear like this.

Tips and tricks appear like this.

Get in touch

Feedback from our readers is always welcome.

General feedback: Email `feedback@packtpub.com` and mention the book title in the subject of your message. If you have questions about any aspect of this book, please email us at `questions@packtpub.com`.

Errata: Although we have taken every care to ensure the accuracy of our content, mistakes do happen. If you have found a mistake in this book, we would be grateful if you would report this to us. Please visit `www.packtpub.com/submit-errata`, selecting your book, clicking on the Errata Submission Form link, and entering the details.

Piracy: If you come across any illegal copies of our works in any form on the Internet, we would be grateful if you would provide us with the location address or website name. Please contact us at `copyright@packtpub.com` with a link to the material.

If you are interested in becoming an author: If there is a topic that you have expertise in and you are interested in either writing or contributing to a book, please visit `authors.packtpub.com`.

Reviews

Please leave a review. Once you have read and used this book, why not leave a review on the site that you purchased it from? Potential readers can then see and use your unbiased opinion to make purchase decisions, we at Packt can understand what you think about our products, and our authors can see your feedback on their book. Thank you!

For more information about Packt, please visit `packtpub.com`.

Introduction to Artificial Intelligence and Java

1

In this chapter, we'll be talking about what machine learning is, why we do machine learning, what supervised learning is, and what unsupervised learning is. We will also understand the difference between classification and regression. Following this, we will start with the installation of JDK and JRE, and will also set up NetBeans on our system. Toward the end of the chapter, we will download and use a JAR file for our project.

Therefore, we will be covering the following topics in this chapter:

- What is machine learning?
- Difference between classification and regression
- Installing JDK and JRE
- Setting up the NetBeans IDE
- Importing Java libraries and exporting code in projects as a JAR file

Let's get started and see what the AI problems that are related to supervised and unsupervised learning are.

What is machine learning?

The capability of **machine learning** is actually the capability of adding new knowledge, or refining previous knowledge, that will help us in making the best or optimum decisions. Note the following, according to the economist and political scientist, *Herbert Simon:*

> *"Learning is any process by which a system improves performance from experience."*

There is a standard definition that has been given by *Tom Mitchell*, who is a computer scientist and E. Fredkin University Professor at the **Carnegie Mellon University (CMU)**, that is as follows:

"A program is said to learn from experience E with respect to some class of task T and performance measure P. If its performance at tasks in T, as measured by P, improves with experience E, then it is machine learning."

What this means is that when we have certain data and experiences available to us along with the help of a human expert, we are able to classify that particular data. For example, let's say we have some emails. With the help of a human, we can filter the emails as spam, business, marketing, and so on. This means that we are classifying our emails based on our experiences and classes of task T are the classes/filters that we have assigned to the emails.

With this data in mind, if we train our model, we can make a model that will classify emails according to our preferences. This is machine learning. We can always check whether the system has learned perfectly or not, which would be considered as a performance measure.

In this way, we will receive more data in the form of emails and we will be able to classify them, and it would be an improvement of the data. With that gained experience from the new data, the system's performance would improve.

This is the basic idea of machine learning.

The question is, why are we actually doing this?

We do this because we want to develop systems that are too difficult or expensive to construct manually – whether that's because they require specific detailed skills or knowledge tuned to a specific task. This is known as a **knowledge engineering bottleneck**. As humans, we don't have enough time to actually develop rules for each and every thing, so we look at data and we learn from data in order to make our systems predict things based on learning from data.

The following diagram illustrates the basic architecture of a learning system:

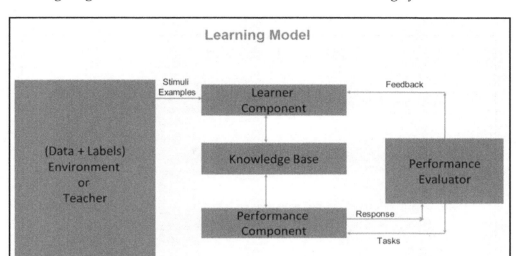

In the preceding diagram, we have a **Teacher**, we have **Data**, and we add **Labels** onto them, and we also have a **Teacher** who has assigned these labels. We give it to a **Learner Component**, which keeps it in a **Knowledge Base**, from which we can evaluate its performance and send it to a **Performance Component**. Here, we can have different evaluation measures, which we'll look at in future chapter, using which we can send **Feedback** to the **Learner Component**. This process can be improved and built upon over time.

The following diagram illustrates a basic architecture of how our supervised learning system looks:

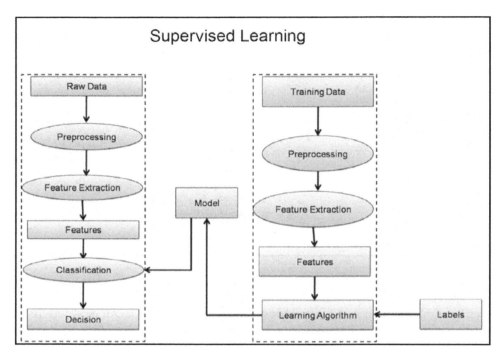

Suppose we have some **Training Data**. Based on that, we can do some **Preprocessing** and extract features that are important. These **Features** will be given to a **Learning Algorithm** with some **Labels** attached that have been assigned by a human expert. This algorithm will then learn and create a **Model**. Once the **Model** has been created, we can take the new data, preprocess it, and extract features from it; based on those **Features**, we then send the data to a **Model**, which will do some kind of a **Classification** before providing a **Decision**. When we complete this process, and when we have a human who provides us with **Labels**, this kind of learning is known as **supervised learning**.

On the other hand, there is unsupervised learning, which is illustrated in the following diagram:

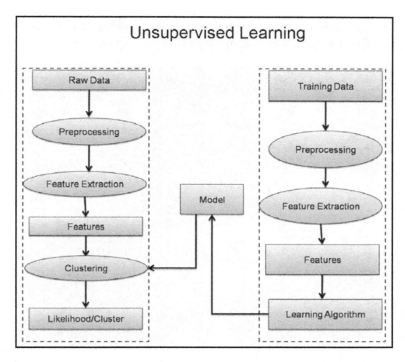

In unsupervised learning, we extract data and later **Features** before giving it to a **Learning Algorithm**, but there is no kind of human intervention that provides classification. In this case, the machine would group the data into smaller clusters, which is how the **Model** will learn. The next time features are extracted and given to a **Model**, the **Model** will provide us with four emails that belong to cluster 1, five emails that belong to cluster 3, and so on. This is known as **unsupervised learning**, and the algorithms that we use are known as **clustering algorithms**.

Differences between classification and regression

In our classification system, we have data that is used to train our model. In this case of sorting emails into clusters, discrete values are provided with the data, and this is known as **classification**.

There is another aspect of supervised learning, where instead of providing a discrete value, we provide it with a continuous value. This is known as **regression**. Regression is also considered supervised learning. The difference between classification and regression is that the first has discrete values and the latter has continuous, numeric values. The following diagram illustrates the three learning algorithms that we can use:

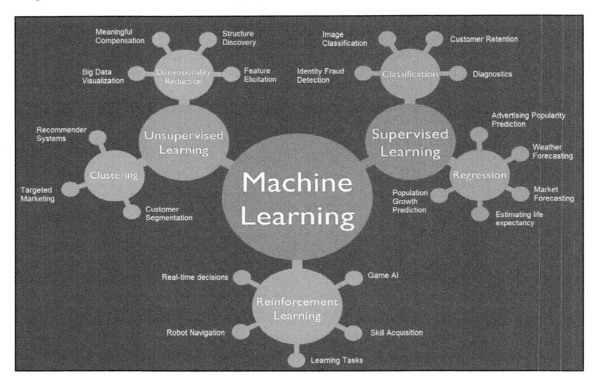

As you can see in the preceding diagram, we use **Supervised Learning, Unsupervised Learning**, and **Reinforcement Learning**. When we talk about **Supervised Learning**, we also use **Classification**. Within **Classification**, we perform tasks such as **Identify Fraud Detection, Image Classification, Customer Retention**, and **Diagnostics**. In **Regression**, we perform activities such as **Advertising Popularity Prediction, Weather Forecasting**, and so on. In **Reinforcement**, we perform **Game AI, Skill Acquisition**, and so on. Finally, in **Unsupervised Learning**, we have **Recommender Systems** and different sub-fields of machine learning, as illustrated.

Installing JDK and JRE

Since we will be coding in Java, we will need the **Java Development Kit (JDK)**. JDK is an environment that comprises a compiler and an interpreter. The compiler is used to convert source code that is written in a high-level language into an intermediate form, which is byte code. That means that the JDK compiles the entire code and converts it into byte code. Once you have byte code, you need a Java interpreter, which is known as a **Java Runtime Environment (JRE)**. JRE provides you with just the Java interpreter. If you have a JRE and byte code, you can run it on your system, as shown in the following diagram:

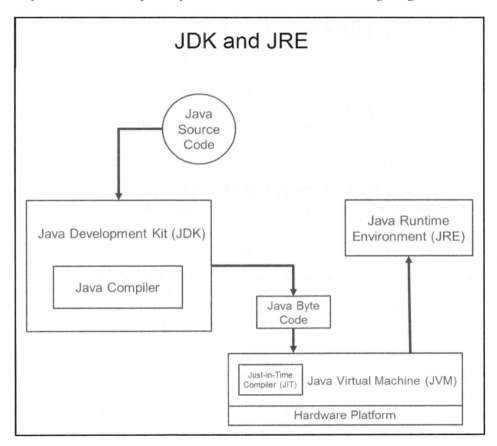

We will now download JDK onto our system.

Open your browser and go to the link https://www.oracle.com/technetwork/java/javase/downloads/index.html. Here, you will get an option to download Java. Currently, JDK 8 is supported by NetBeans. We have JDK 10, but it's not supporting NetBeans. If you don't have NetBeans in JDK, go to http://www.oracle.com/technetwork/java/javase/downloads/jdk-netbeans-jsp-142931.html. You have to accept the agreement, and based on your system, you can then download NetBeans and JDK, as shown in the following screenshot:

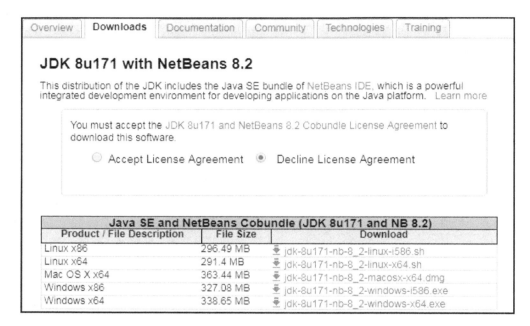

If you only want to install JDK, you have to go to JDK 8 at `http://www.oracle.com/technetwork/java/javase/downloads/jdk8-downloads-2133151.html`. It will take you to the next page where you will also find more information about JDK 8, as follows:

Java SE Development Kit 8u181

You must accept the Oracle Binary Code License Agreement for Java SE to download this software.

   ◯ Accept License Agreement   ◯ Decline License Agreement

Product / File Description	File Size	Download
Linux ARM 32 Hard Float ABI	72.95 MB	⬇ jdk-8u181-linux-arm32-vfp-hflt.tar.gz
Linux ARM 64 Hard Float ABI	69.89 MB	⬇ jdk-8u181-linux-arm64-vfp-hflt.tar.gz
Linux x86	165.06 MB	⬇ jdk-8u181-linux-i586.rpm
Linux x86	179.87 MB	⬇ jdk-8u181-linux-i586.tar.gz
Linux x64	162.15 MB	⬇ jdk-8u181-linux-x64.rpm
Linux x64	177.05 MB	⬇ jdk-8u181-linux-x64.tar.gz
Mac OS X x64	242.83 MB	⬇ jdk-8u181-macosx-x64.dmg
Solaris SPARC 64-bit (SVR4 package)	133.17 MB	⬇ jdk-8u181-solaris-sparcv9.tar.Z
Solaris SPARC 64-bit	94.34 MB	⬇ jdk-8u181-solaris-sparcv9.tar.gz
Solaris x64 (SVR4 package)	133.83 MB	⬇ jdk-8u181-solaris-x64.tar.Z
Solaris x64	92.11 MB	⬇ jdk-8u181-solaris-x64.tar.gz
Windows x86	194.41 MB	⬇ jdk-8u181-windows-i586.exe
Windows x64	202.73 MB	⬇ jdk-8u181-windows-x64.exe

Now, you have to accept the agreement again and download JDK according to your system requirements.

Once you have downloaded JDK, it is easy to install. For Windows and macOS, you just have to right-click on it. For Linux machines, you can either use a `sudo` or `apt-get` command on Ubuntu.

Setting up the NetBeans IDE

We will now download NetBeans onto our system. Visit the link at `https://netbeans.org/ downloads/`. You should see something like the following screenshot:

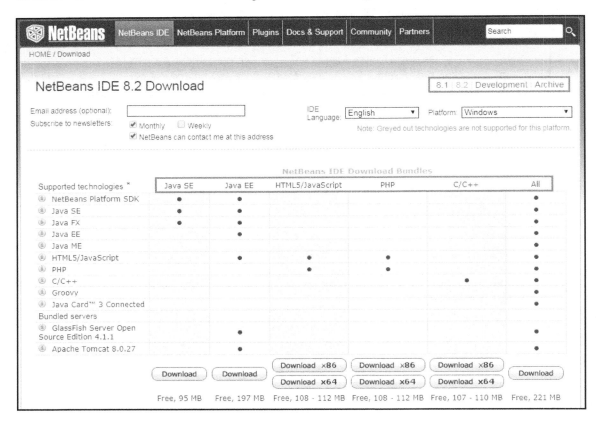

Here, you will find information about the current NetBeans version, which is NetBeans 8.2. You can download either **Java SE**, **Java EE**, or any other **NetBeans IDE Download Bundle**. It is advisable that you download the **All** bundle because it supports all of the technologies, as seen in the preceding screenshot. You never know when you might need them!

As shown on the top-right corner, **8.2** is the current version that you will be downloading. If you don't want to download this version, you can download its immediate predecessor, which is **8.1**. If you want to download the experimental versions, which are the alpha or beta versions, click on **Development**. If you want to download versions that are earlier than **8.1**, you can go to **Archive**, and this will help you in downloading the required version, as seen in the following screenshot:

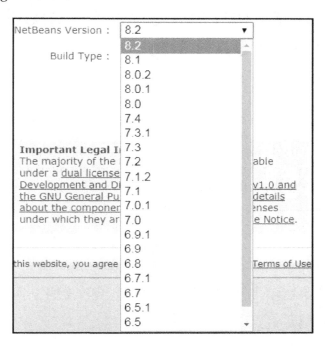

As shown in the preceding diagram, **8.2** is the latest version of NetBeans. There have been changes in subsequent versions of NetBeans, but we will be using **8.2**. You can download older versions if you want. Versions such as **7.1** and **7.0.1**, for example, work in a different way but can be used with older Java code.

Once you have downloaded NetBeans, you will get an .exe file on Windows. You just have to double-click on it and follow the instructions to install it. On a Mac, it will appear as a .dmg file; just click on it to install it. The installation process is simple, as you simply have to follow the prompts. On Linux, you will get a .sh file. Here, simply run the shell script and click on **Next** to proceed. NetBeans should now be installed on your machine!

Before installing NetBeans, make sure you have JDK installed. If not, you will get an error and NetBeans will not install on your system.

Importing Java libraries and exporting code in projects as a JAR file

We will now download a JAR file from the internet and use it in our project to create a JAR file for our project.

Open a web browser and search for download a junit.jar. This will take you to a link where you can download a JAR file. There are online repositories available where JAR files exist. One of the most reliable repositories can be found at http://www.java2s.com/Code/Jar/j/Downloadjunitjar.htm, where you can download any available JAR file. If you click on it, it should take you to the following page:

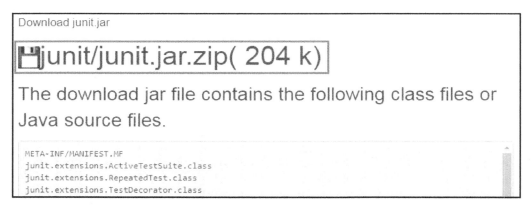

As seen in the preceding screenshot, you will find the junit.jar file and the different classes that are available in the JAR file also listed. You can right-click on the save (floppy disc) symbol to save the file on your system.

Once the file is downloaded, extract it into a `junit.jar` file. You can then add it to your project with the following steps:

1. Create a new project on NetBeans, for example, **HelloWorld**.
2. Since the new project will not have the `junit.jar` file, go to **Properties** by right-clicking on the project, as shown in the following screenshot:

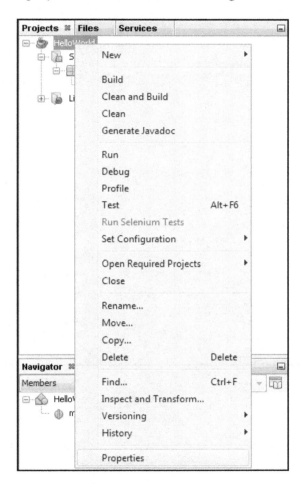

3. Go to the **Libraries** | **Add JAR/Folder** option and provide the location of where this `junit.jar` file is, as follows:

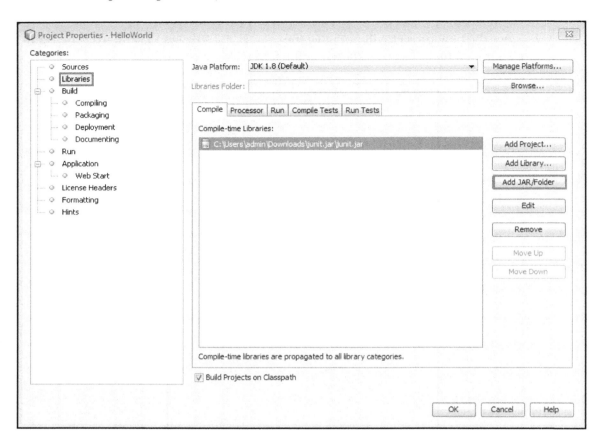

4. Once done, click on **Open** and it will be added to your project:

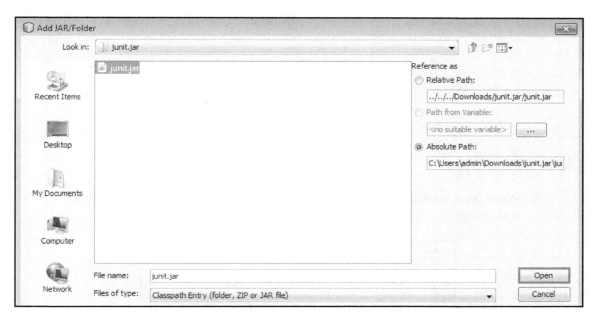

5. Now the JAR file has been added to the project, we can use the `junit.jar` file in an `import` statement. We can also `import` individual packages, as shown in the following screenshot:

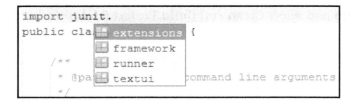

6. If you want to use all of the classes in `framework`, you just have to write the following code:

```
import junit.framework.*;
```

7. Now, let's use the following code to print the output `Hello World`:

```
package helloworld;

/**
```

```
    *
    * @author admin
    */
import junit.framework.*;
public class HelloWorld {

    /**
    * @param args the command line arguments
    */
    public static void main(String[] args) {
    // TODO code application logic here
    System.out.println("Hello World");
    }
}
```

8. After running the preceding code, you should get an output similar to the following:

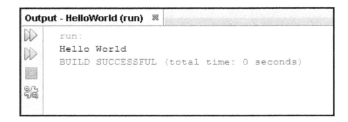

If you want to create a JAR file for this project, please perform the following steps:

1. Go to **Run** and select **Clean and Build Project (HelloWorld)** to build your project:

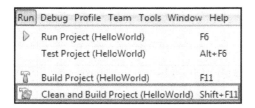

2. Once building the `HelloWorld` project is complete, the **Output** window will say BUILD SUCCESSFUL, as shown in the following screenshot:

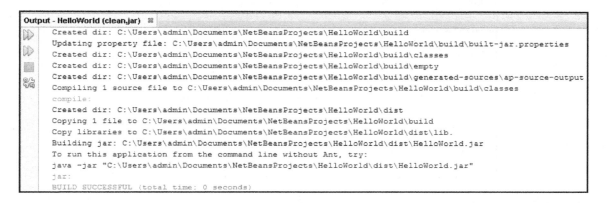

3. To check if the JAR file been created or not, go to Windows Explorer and navigate to your project's location, which you received from the previous output:

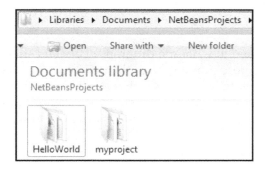

4. Open the project folder, in our case `HelloWorld`, and go into the `dist` folder, as follows:

5. In the `dist` folder, you will find the JAR file (`HelloWorld.jar`), which you can use and where there will be a `lib` folder. This will contain the `junit.jar` file that is being used by the `HelloWorld.jar` file:

This means that whenever you use any JAR files in your project, they will be stored in the `lib` folder of your JAR file.

Summary

In this chapter, we first looked at what the difference between supervised and unsupervised learning is, before moving on to the difference between classification and regression. We then saw how to install JDK, what the difference between JDK and JRE is, and how to install a NetBeans IDE. We also created our own JAR file by importing another JAR file into our project. In the next chapter, we'll learn how to search and explore different search algorithms.

2
Exploring Search Algorithms

In this chapter, we'll look at how to perform a search, and we will cover the basic requirements of implementing a search algorithm. We'll then practice by implementing Dijkstra's algorithm, before moving on to heuristics, showing how they can be used in search algorithms to improve the accuracy of search results.

In particular, we'll be focusing on the following topics:

- An introduction to searching
- Implementing Dijkstra's search
- Understanding the notion of heuristics
- A brief introduction to the A* algorithm
- Implementing an A* algorithm

An introduction to searching

Let's look at what it means to search. If we want to apply a search to any problem, we will need four pieces of input, which are referred to as the state space, and are as follows:

[S, s, O, G]

The preceding types of input can be described as follows:

- **S**: A set of implicitly given states—all of the states that might be explored in a search process.
- **s**: The start symbol—the starting point of the search.
- **O**: The state transition operators, which indicate how a search should proceed from one node to the next and what transitions are available to the search. This is an exhaustive list. Therefore, the state transition operator keeps track of these exhaustive lists.
- **G**: The goal node, pointing to where the search should end.

With the preceding information, we can find the following values:

- The minimum cost transaction for a goal state
- A sequence of transitions to a minimum cost goal
- A minimum cost transaction for a minimum cost goal

Let's consider the following algorithm, which assumes that all operators have a cost:

1. Initialize: Set $OPEN = \{s\}$,

   $CLOSE = \{\}$, Set $C(s) = 0$

2. Fail: If $OPEN = \{\}$, Terminate with Failure
3. Select: Select the minimum cost state, n, form $OPEN$, and Save n in $CLOSE$
4. Terminate: If $n \in G$, Terminate with Success
5. Expand: Generate the successors of n using 0

   For each successor, m, insert m in $OPEN$ only if $m \notin [OPEN \cup CLOSE]$

   Set $C(m) = C(n) + C(n,m)$

   and insert m in $OPEN$

   if $m \in [OPEN \cup CLOSE]$

   Set $C(m) = min\{ C(m), C(n) + C(m,n)\}$

   If $C(m)$ has decreased and $m \in CLOSE$ move it to $OPEN$

6. Loop: Go to Step 2

Each state of the preceding algorithm can be described as follows:

1. **Initialize**: We initialize the algorithm and create a data structure called *OPEN*. We put our start state, s, into this data structure, and create one more data structure, *CLOSE*, which is empty. All of the states that we'll be exploring will be taken from *OPEN* and put into *CLOSE*. We set the cost of the initial start state to 0. This will calculate the cost incurred when traveling from the start state to the current state. The cost of traveling from the start state to the start state is 0; that's why we have set it to 0.

2. **Fail**: In this step, if *OPEN* is empty, we will terminate with a failure. However, our *OPEN* is not empty, because we have s in our start state. Therefore, we will not terminate with a failure.

3. **Select state**: Here, we will select the minimum cost successor, *n*, and we'll take it from *OPEN* and save it in *CLOSE*.
4. **Terminate**: In this step, we'll check whether *n* belongs to the *G*. If yes, we'll terminate with a success.
5. **Expand**: If our *n* does not belong to *G*, then we need to expand *G* by using our state transition operator, as follows:
    - If it is a new node, *m*, and we have not explored it, it means that it is not available in either *OPEN* or *CLOSE*, and we'll simply calculate the cost of the new successor (*m*) by calculating the cost of its predecessor plus the cost of traveling from *n* to *m*, and we'll put the value into *OPEN*
    - If it is a part of both *OPEN* and *CLOSE*, we'll check which one is the minimum cost—the current cost or the previous cost (the actual cost that we had in the previous iteration)—and we'll keep that cost
    - If our *m* gets decreased and it belongs to *CLOSE*, then we will bring it back to *OPEN*
6. **Loop**: We will keep on doing this until our *OPEN* is not empty, or until our *m* does not belong to *G*.

Consider the example illustrated in the following diagram:

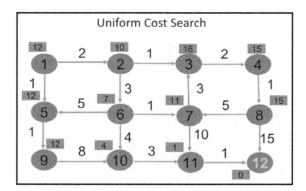

Initially, we have the following algorithm:

$$n(S) = 12 \mid s = 1 \mid G = \{12\}$$

In the preceding algorithm, the following applies:

- *n(S)* is the number of states/nodes
- *s* is the start node
- *G* is the goal node

The arrows are the state transition operators. Let's try running this, in order to check that our algorithm is working.

Iteration 1 of the algorithm is as follows:

Step 1: *OPEN = {1}, C(1) = 0 | CLOSE = { }*; here *C(1)* is cost of node *1*

Step 2: *OPEN ≠ { }*; go to Step 3

Step 3: *n = 1 | OPEN = { } | CLOSE = {1}*

Step 4: Since *n ∉ G*; Expand *n=1*

We get *m = {2, 5}*

{2} ∉ [OPEN ∪ CLOSE] | {5} ∉ [OPEN ∪ CLOSE]

C(2) = 0 + 2 = 2 | C(5) = 0 + 1 = 1 | OPEN = {2,5}

Loop to Step 2

Iteration 2 is as follows:

Step 2: *OPEN ≠ { }* so Step 3

Step 3: *n = 5* since *min{C(2),C(5)} = C(5)*, that is, *1 | OPEN = {2} | CLOSE = {1,5}*

Step 4: *n ∉ G* so Step Expand

Step Expand *n = 5 : m = {9}*

{9} ∉ [OPEN ∪ CLOSE]

C(9) = 1 + 1 = 2 | OPEN = {2,9}

Loop to Step 2

Iteration 3 is as follows:

Step 2: *OPEN ≠ { }* so Step 3

Step 3: $n = 2$ with preference to *2(2)* since it came first | *OPEN = {9}* | *CLOSE = {1,5,2}*

Step 4: $n \notin G$ so Step Expand

Step Expand $n = 2 : m = \{6,3\}$

$\{6\} \notin [OPEN \cup CLOSE]$ | $\{3\} \notin [OPEN \cup CLOSE]$

$C(6) = 2 + 3 = 5$ | $C(3) = 2 + 1 = 3$ | *OPEN = {9,6,3}*

Loop to Step 2

Iteration 4 is as follows:

Step 2: *OPEN ≠ { }* so Step 3

Step 3: $n = 9$ since $min\{C(9),C(6),C(3)\} = C(9)$, that is, 2 | *OPEN = {6,3}* | *CLOSE = {1,5,2,9}*

Step 4: $n \notin G$ so Step Expand

Step Expand $n = 9 : m = \{10\}$

$\{10\} \notin [OPEN \cup CLOSE]$

$C(10) = 2 + 8 = 10$ | *OPEN = {6,3,10}*

Loop to Step 2

Iteration 5 is as follows:

Step 2: *OPEN ≠ { }* so Step 3

Step 3: $n = 3$ since $min\{C(6),C(3),C(10)\} = C(3)$, that is, 3 | *OPEN = {6,10}* | *CLOSE = {1,5,2,9,3}*

Step 4: $n \notin G$ so Step Expand

Step Expand $n = 3 : m = \{4\}$

$\{4\} \notin [OPEN \cup CLOSE]$

$C(4) = 3 + 2 = 5 \mid OPEN = \{6,10,4\}$

Loop to Step 2

Iteration 6 is as follows:

Step 2: $OPEN \neq \{ \}$ so Step 3

Step 3: $n = 6$ with preference to $6(5)$ since it came first $\mid OPEN = \{10,4\} \mid CLOSE = \{1,5,2,9,3,6\}$

Step 4: $n \notin G$ so Step Expand

Step Expand $n = 6 : m = \{5,10,7\}$

$\{5\} \in [OPEN \cup CLOSE] \mid \{10\} \in [OPEN \cup CLOSE] \mid \{7\} \notin [OPEN \cup CLOSE]$

$C(7) = 5 + 1 = 6 \mid OPEN = \{10,4,7\}$

$C(5) = min\{C(5), C(6,5)\} = min\{1, 5 + 5 = 10\} = 1$

$C(10) = min\{C(10), C(6,10)\} = min\{10, 6 + 4 = 9\} = 9 \mid$ Since $C(10)$ has decreased check if C is part of $OPEN$

Loop to Step 2

Iteration 7 is as follows:

Step 2: $OPEN \neq \{ \}$ so Step 3

Step 3: $n = 4$ since $min\{C(10),C(4),C(7)\} = C(4)$, that is, $5 \mid OPEN = \{10,7\} \mid CLOSE = \{1,5,2,9,3,6,4\}$

Step 4: $n \notin G$ so Step Expand

Step Expand $n = 4 : m = \{8\}$

$\{8\} \notin [OPEN \cup CLOSE]$

$C(8) = 5 + 1 = 6 \mid OPEN = \{10,7,8\}$

Loop to Step 2

Iteration 8 is as follows:

Step 2: *OPEN ≠ { }* so Step 3

Step 3: $n = 7$ since $min\{C(10),C(7),C(8)\} = C(7)$, that is, 6 | $OPEN = \{10,8\}$ | $CLOSE = \{1,5,2,9,3,6,4,7\}$

Step 4: $n \notin G$ so Step Expand

Step Expand $n = 7 : m = \{11\}$

$\{11\} \notin [OPEN \cup CLOSE]$

$C(11) = 6 + 10 = 16$ | $OPEN = \{10,8,11\}$

Loop to Step 2

Iteration 9 is as follows:

Step 2: *OPEN ≠ { }* so Step 3

Step 3: $n = 8$ since $min\{C(10),C(8),C(11)\} = C(8)$, that is, 6 | $OPEN = \{10,11\}$ | $CLOSE = \{1,5,2,9,3,6,4,7,8\}$

Step 4: $n \notin G$ so Step Expand

Step Expand $n = 8 : m = \{12,7\}$

$\{12\} \notin [OPEN \cup CLOSE]$ | $\{7\} \in [OPEN \cup CLOSE]$

$C(12) = 6 + 15 = 21$ | $OPEN = \{10,11,12\}$

$C(7) = min\{C(7), C(8,7)\} = min\{6, 6 + 5 = 11\} = 6$

Loop to Step 2

Iteration 10 is as follows:

Step 2: *OPEN ≠ { }* so Step 3

Step 3: $n = 10$ since $min\{C(10),C(11),C(12)\} = C(10)$, that is, 9 | $OPEN = \{11,12\}$ | $CLOSE = \{1,5,2,9,3,6,4,7,8,10\}$

Step 4: $n \notin G$ so Step Expand

Step Expand $n = 10 : m = \{11\}$

$\{11\} \in [OPEN \cup CLOSE]$

$C(11) = min\{C(11), C(10,11)\} = min\{16, 9 + 3 = 12\} = 12$

Loop to Step 2

Iteration 11 is as follows:

Step 2: $OPEN \neq \{ \}$ so Step 3

Step 3: $n = 11$ since $min\{C(11),C(12)\} = C(11)$, that is, 12 | $OPEN = \{12\}$ | $CLOSE = \{1,5,2,9,3,6,4,7,8,10,11\}$

Step 4: $n \notin G$ so Step Expand

Step Expand $n = 11 : m = \{12\}$

$\{12\} \in [OPEN \cup CLOSE]$

$C(12) = min\{C(12), C(11,12)\} = min\{21, 12 + 1 = 13\} = 13$

Loop to Step 2

Iteration 12 is as follows:

Step 2: $OPEN \neq \{ \}$ so Step 3

Step 3: $n = 12$ | $OPEN = \{\}$ | $CLOSE = \{1,5,2,9,3,6,4,7,8,10,11,12\}$

Step 4: $n \in G$ so Terminate with Success

Since n belongs to our goal node, we'll terminate with a success, and this will end our search.

Implementing Dijkstra's search

Now, we will look at the code for Dijkstra's search algorithm, which we discussed in the *An introduction to searching* section.

Let's get straight to the code, and look at how it works. In the previous section, the very first thing that we showed were the vertices; each vertex had certain properties. We will now create a `Vertex` class, as follows:

```
public class Vertex {
    final private String id;
    final private String name;

    public Vertex(String id, String name) {
        this.id = id;
        this.name = name;
    }

    @Override
    public int hashCode() {
        final int prime = 31;
        int result = 1;
        result = prime * result + ((id == null) ? 0 : id.hashCode());
        return result;
    }

    @Override
    public boolean equals(Object obj) {
        if (this == obj)
            return true;
        if (obj == null)
            return false;
        if (getClass() != obj.getClass())
            return false;
        Vertex other = (Vertex) obj;
        if (id == null) {
            if (other.id != null)
                return false;
        } else if (!id.equals(other.id))
            return false;
        return true;
    }
    @Override
    public String toString() {
        return name;
    }
}
```

The `Vertex` class will take two values: the `id` and the `name`. Then, we'll include a constructor (to assign the values) and the `hashCode()` method (which will print the values).

Then, we will override an `equals` object, to see whether our two objects are equal. If an object is `null`, we will return `false`; otherwise, we'll return `true`. If we don't have that particular class, or if we don't have the object for the class, we will return `false`. This will be done to check our position (whether we are at the end of the graph), if there are more outgoing nodes, and so on.

The `toString()` method will print the name of the vertex.

Then, we will have the `Edge` class, as follows:

```
public class Edge {
    private final String id;
    private final Vertex source;
    private final Vertex destination;
    private final int weight;
```

The `Edge` class has a starting vertex and an ending vertex. Therefore, we will now have a starting vertex (`source`) and an ending vertex (`destination`), and each `Edge` will have an `id`. Each `Edge` will also have a certain value (a cost associated with it), and we will store that in the `weight` variable, as follows:

```
public Edge(String id, Vertex source, Vertex destination, int weight) {
    this.id = id;
    this.source = source;
    this.destination = destination;
    this.weight = weight;
}
public String getId() {
    return id;
}
public Vertex getDestination() {
    return destination;
}

public Vertex getSource() {
    return source;
}
public int getWeight() {
    return weight;
}
//@Override
public String toString() {
    return source + " " + destination;
}
}
}
```

The `Edge` class constructor will initialize the `getId()`, `getDestination()`, `getSource()`, and `getWeight()` values, and they will all print their corresponding values. We will then override the `toString()` method, where we will print the `source` in the target `destination`.

Once we have done so, we'll create a `Graph` class, as follows:

```java
import java.util.List;

public class Graph {
    private final List<Vertex> vertexes;
    private final List<Edge> edges;

    public Graph(List<Vertex> vertexes, List<Edge> edges) {
        this.vertexes = vertexes;
        this.edges = edges;
    }

    public List<Vertex> getVertexes() {
        return vertexes;
    }

    public List<Edge> getEdges() {
        return edges;
    }
}
```

The `Graph` class will import the `util.List` class, and it will assign a `List<Vertex>` and an `List<Edge>` in the `vertexes` and `edges` variables. The `Graph` class constructor will initialize these values, and the `getVertexes()` method will return the `vertexes`. The `getEdges()` method will return the `edges`, which will be of the `Vertex` type of the `List C` type.

We are now ready to implement our Dijkstra's algorithm. We'll `import` the following classes:

```java
import java.util.ArrayList;
import java.util.Collections;
import java.util.HashMap;
import java.util.HashSet;
import java.util.LinkedList;
import java.util.List;
import java.util.Map;
import java.util.Set;
```

Then, we'll create constraints with `List` and `edges`, as follows:

```
public class DijkstraAlgorithm {

    private final List<Vertex> nodes;
    private final List<Edge> edges;
    private Set<Vertex> close;
    private Set<Vertex> open;
    private Map<Vertex, Vertex> predecessors;
    private Map<Vertex, Integer> distance;
```

We have created a set of vertices (`Set<Vertex>`) for our two data structures, `open` and `close`. Then, we have the `Map`, where we'll keep a record of all of the predecessors of our current node. Therefore, we'll have `Map<Vertex, Vertex>`, which will take `predecessors`, and we'll also have the cost (`distance`). Hence, we'll have `Vertex` and `Integer`, which will keep track of the cost of a particular `Vertex`.

The `this` constructor will initialize the
`ArrayList<Vertex>(graph.getVertexes())` and
`ArrayList<Edge>(graph.getEdges())` values, and will take `graph` as an object. The `graph` object will return our vertices and edges, and `getVertexes()` will return our vertices and edges, which will be cast to an `ArrayList` and assigned to `nodes` and `edges`:

```
public DijkstraAlgorithm(Graph graph) {
    // create a copy of the array so that we can operate on this array
    this.nodes = new ArrayList<Vertex>(graph.getVertexes());
    this.edges = new ArrayList<Edge>(graph.getEdges());
}
```

The `close` and `open` objects are of the type `HashSet`, and `distance` is initialized to `HashMap` values. We'll initialize these values; initially, we will put the source value as 0, and we will assign this starting point to an `open` data structure, or an `open` set. We will do this until our `open` set is not empty. If our `open` set is not empty, we will create a node of the `Vertex` type, and we'll get the minimum of all of the nodes. Therefore, `getMinimum()` will go through the vertices that we have in `open`, in order to find which one is of the minimum value. Once we have a node from `open`, we'll assign it to `close`, and we'll remove it from `open`. Then, we'll find the descendants of our particular node, and we'll find their minimum value, as follows:

```
public void execute(Vertex source) {
    close = new HashSet<Vertex>();
    open = new HashSet<Vertex>();
    distance = new HashMap<Vertex, Integer>();
    predecessors = new HashMap<Vertex, Vertex>();
    distance.put(source, 0);
```

```
    open.add(source);
    while (open.size() > 0) {
        Vertex node = getMinimum(open);
        close.add(node);
        open.remove(node);
        findMinimalDistances(node);
    }
}
```

The following code will find the minimum values and add the values to the target:

```
private void findMinimalDistances(Vertex node) {
    List<Vertex> adjacentNodes = getNeighbors(node);
    for (Vertex target : adjacentNodes) {
        if (getShortestDistance(target) > getShortestDistance(node)
                + getDistance(node, target)) {
            distance.put(target, getShortestDistance(node)
                    + getDistance(node, target));
            predecessors.put(target, node);
            open.add(target);
        }
    }
}
```

The `getDistance()` method fetches the distance of a particular `node`, and also the distance from a `node` to the `target`. Therefore, we will pass those two values, `node` and `target`, and the values will be added to the `weight`. The `getWeight()` method will get the `weight`, and it will get assigned to the same. We'll add them to the `target`, and we'll then have the `node` value plus its own `weight`, which we will get via the `getWeight()` method:

```
private int getDistance(Vertex node, Vertex target) {
    for (Edge edge : edges) {
        if (edge.getSource().equals(node)
                && edge.getDestination().equals(target)) {
            return edge.getWeight();
        }
    }
    throw new RuntimeException("Should not happen");
}
```

We also have the `getNeighbors()` method. Here, all of the neighbors will be printed, as follows:

```
private List<Vertex> getNeighbors(Vertex node) {
    List<Vertex> neighbors = new ArrayList<Vertex>();
    for (Edge edge : edges) {
```

```
        if (edge.getSource().equals(node)
                && !isSettled(edge.getDestination())) {
            neighbors.add(edge.getDestination());
        }
    }
    return neighbors;
}
```

The `getMinimum()` method will check all of the available values that are in `open`, and will pass the value to `vertexes`. From `vertexes`, we'll check for the `minimum` value, and then we will `return` it:

```
    private Vertex getMinimum(Set<Vertex> vertexes) {
        Vertex minimum = null;
        for (Vertex vertex : vertexes) {
            if (minimum == null) {
                minimum = vertex;
            } else {
                if (getShortestDistance(vertex) <
getShortestDistance(minimum)) {
                    minimum = vertex;
                }
            }
        }
        return minimum;
    }

    private boolean isSettled(Vertex vertex) {
        return close.contains(vertex);
    }
```

We also have the `getShortestDistance` method. This will get the shortest distance from a particular node and pass it. With the result, we can check the minimum distance:

```
    private int getShortestDistance(Vertex destination) {
        Integer d = distance.get(destination);
        if (d == null) {
            return Integer.MAX_VALUE;
        } else {
            return d;
        }
    }
```

Similarly, the `getPath` method will get the most optimal path from a node, as follows:

```
    public LinkedList<Vertex> getPath(Vertex target) {
        LinkedList<Vertex> path = new LinkedList<Vertex>();
        Vertex step = target;
```

```
    // check if a path exists
    if (predecessors.get(step) == null) {
        return null;
    }
    path.add(step);
    while (predecessors.get(step) != null) {
        step = predecessors.get(step);
        path.add(step);
    }
    // Put it into the correct order
    Collections.reverse(path);
    return path;
  }

}
```

Now, we will create our `Test` class, where we will `import` the following classes:

```
import java.util.ArrayList;
import java.util.LinkedList;
import java.util.List;

import static org.junit.Assert.assertNotNull;
import static org.junit.Assert.assertTrue;
```

In order to `import` the `assertNotNull` and `assertTrue` classes from the `junit` package, we need to import the `junit.jar` and `hamcrest-core-1.3.jar` packages. We will do this by going into our project and right-clicking on it, arriving at **Properties**. In **Properties**, we'll go to **Libraries** and click on **Add JAR/Folder**, and we will provide the path to the JAR files, as shown in the following screenshot:

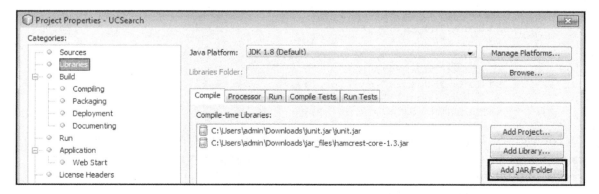

First, we'll create the `nodes` and `edges`, and then we'll initialize them. Then, we'll provide the entire input graph, as follows:

```
public class Test {

    private List<Vertex> nodes;
    private List<Edge> edges;

    public void testExcute() {
        nodes = new ArrayList<Vertex>();
        edges = new ArrayList<Edge>();
        for (int i = 0; i < 12; i++) {
            Vertex location = new Vertex("Node_" + i, "Node_" + i);
            nodes.add(location);
        }
```

In the preceding example, we had 12 `nodes`, so we'll initialize them from 0 to 11. We will use a `for` loop from `i = 0` to `i < 12`, and we'll create a `location` object for `Vertex` and add the `nodes` to the `location`.

The `addLane` method will have the edges, as shown in the following code snippet:

```
addLane("Edge_0", 0, 1, 2);
addLane("Edge_1", 0, 4, 1);
addLane("Edge_2", 1, 2, 1);
addLane("Edge_3", 1, 5, 3);
addLane("Edge_4", 2, 3, 2);
addLane("Edge_5", 3, 7, 1);
addLane("Edge_6", 4, 8, 1);
addLane("Edge_7", 5, 4, 5);
addLane("Edge_8", 5, 6, 1);
addLane("Edge_9", 5, 9, 4);
addLane("Edge_10", 6, 2, 3);
addLane("Edge_11", 6, 10, 10);
addLane("Edge_12", 7, 11, 15);
addLane("Edge_13", 8, 9, 8);
addLane("Edge_14", 9, 10, 3);
addLane("Edge_15", 10, 11, 1);
addLane("Edge_16", 7, 6, 5);
```

As you can see, in the preceding code, we are taking the values from 0 to 11; in the example, we had edges from 1 to 12. This means that the first vertex that we had is the 0th vertex, and the twelfth vertex that we had is the eleventh vertex in the preceding code. The preceding code snippet includes the following:

```
addLane("Edge ID", source, destination, cost)
```

Therefore, from the 0th vertex to the first vertex, the cost is 2, and from the 0th vertex to the fourth vertex, the cost is 1, and so on. This is how the costs have been defined.

Next, we will initialize a `graph` object, which we will pass the `nodes` and `edges` to. We will then assign the `graph` object to our `dijkstra` object and call the `dijkstra.execute` method, assigning the first node to the `execute` method. Hence, the `getSource` method will have the very first value that we had. Finally, the vertex `getPath` will get the entire path, as follows:

```
Graph graph = new Graph(nodes, edges);
DijkstraAlgorithm dijkstra = new DijkstraAlgorithm(graph);
dijkstra.execute(nodes.get(0));
LinkedList<Vertex> path = dijkstra.getPath(nodes.get(10));

assertNotNull(path);
assertTrue(path.size() > 0);

for (Vertex vertex : path) {
    System.out.println(vertex);
}

}
```

Once we have implemented the preceding code, we will use the `addLane` method, as follows:

```
private void addLane(String laneId, int sourceLocNo, int destLocNo,
        int duration) {
    Edge lane = new Edge(laneId, nodes.get(sourceLocNo),
nodes.get(destLocNo), duration );
    edges.add(lane);
}
}
```

The `addLane` method will take four values and call a `lane` object of the `Edge` class. It will initialize the `lane` object, and it will pass the values to that object, which will create the `edges`.

Now, execute the code. You will see the following output:

```
Output - UCSearch (run) %
 run:
 Node_0
 Node_1
 Node_5
 Node_9
 Node_10
 BUILD SUCCESSFUL (total time: 0 seconds)
```

We get the shortest path, which is from `Node_0` to `Node_1` to `Node_5` to `Node_9` to `Node_10`, and the eleventh is our goal node.

In the example in the *An introduction to searching* section, we had the same path, from vertex `1` to `2` to `6` to `10` to `11`, and then, finally, to `12`. This section illustrated Dijkstra's algorithm.

Understanding the notion of heuristics

Let's look at heuristics; later on, we'll look at an example.

Heuristics are an approach to problem solving, learning, and discovery. We apply heuristics when we are not sure of what the goal should be; we can apply certain estimates, and these estimates can help us to optimize our search process. If finding an optimal solution is impossible or impractical, heuristic methods can be used to speed up the process of finding a satisfactory solution.

So, let's look at an example of using heuristics.

Suppose that we have a puzzle with eight tiles, arranged as shown in the **Initial State** cube, and we want to arrange them as they are in the **Goal State** cube:

To take **1** from its **Initial State** to its **Goal State**, we have to move **1** from the first tile to the last tile in the first row.

We also have to move at least two edges (that is, **2** and **3**), so that we can get **1** to its **Goal State** location.

There can be two values: an overestimate and an underestimate. The overestimate is a solution, which is the mechanism, and the underestimate is a mechanism that gets the minimum value from the actual value. So, we can safely say that we need to move at least two tiles to get **1** to its actual position:

Initial State			Goal State		
1	2	3	2	8	1
8		4		4	3
7	6	5	7	6	5

Similarly, we need to move at least one tile to get **2** to its actual position:

Initial State			Goal State		
1	2	3	2	8	1
8		4		4	3
7	6	5	7	6	5

We can also get the heuristic value—the underestimated value of all of the tiles. For example, if we want to move **8** to its **Goal State**, we need to move **1** and **2** by at least two tiles. These are the heuristic values of our tiles, and that is how a heuristic works.

A brief introduction to the A* algorithm

We'll now look at how an A* algorithm works. In this algorithm, we'll calculate two costs. We'll be taking four pieces of input: our start state (a set of implicitly given states), a state transition operator, a goal state, and the heuristic value of each node. Based on those, we'll be calculating our actual cost, $g(n)$ (which we also calculated in our Dijkstra's algorithm). Along with the actual cost, we'll calculate one more cost: the final cost ($f(n)$). The final cost will be the actual cost plus the heuristic cost ($h(n)$). The formula is as follows:

$$f(n) = g(n) + h(n)$$

In the preceding formula, the following applies:

- $g(n)$ is the actual cost of traversing from the initial state to state n
- $h(n)$ is the estimated cost of reaching the goal from state n

We are given the following information:

[S,s,O,G,h]

In the preceding statement, the following applies:

- *S* is an implicitly given set of states
- *s* is the start state
- *O* is the state transition operator
- *G* is the goal
- *h* is the heuristic function on our graph

Our objective is to find the minimum cost, which means that our objective is to find the sequence of transactions, from the start state to the goal state, for the minimum cost. Our algorithm will involve the following steps:

1. Initialize:

   Set *OPEN* ={s},
   CLOSE = {}, *Set f(s) = h(s), g(s) = 0*

2. Fail:

   If *OPEN* = {}, Terminate with Failure

3. Select:

   Select the minimum cost state, *n*, form *OPEN* and Save *n* in *CLOSE*

4. Terminate:

   If $n \in G$, Terminate with Success

5. Expand:

Generate the successors of *n* using *O*. For each successor, *m*, insert *m* in *OPEN* only:

- If $m \notin [OPEN \cup CLOSE]$

  set $g(m) = g(n) + C(n,m)$

  set $f(m) = g(m) + h(m)$

  insert *m* in *OPEN*

- If $m \in [OPEN \cup CLOSE]$

  set $g(m) = min\{g(m), g(n) + C(m,n)\}$

  set $f(m) = g(m) + h(m)$

  If $f(m)$ has decreased and $m \in CLOSE$ move it to *OPEN*

6. Loop:

Go to Step 2.

The preceding algorithm involves the following steps:

1. We import our start state into *OPEN*, and we create a blank data structure called *CLOSE*; we calculate the final state of *s* as the heuristic cost, and our initial, actual cost is 0. Since our actual cost is 0, our heuristic cost will be the final cost.
2. We terminate our search with a failure if our *OPEN* is empty; if not, we'll select the minimum cost state, *n*, from *OPEN*, and we will put that into *CLOSE*. We also performed this in our Dijkstra's search.
3. If our current state is equal to the goal state, we'll terminate with a success.
4. If we do not terminate with a success, we will need to generate the successors of *n*. We'll generate all of the successors of *n* through two mechanisms, as follows:

   - If the particular *m* is not a part of either our *OPEN* or our *CLOSE*, we will calculate the actual cost of *m*, and then we'll calculate the final cost; that will be the actual cost plus the heuristic cost. Then, we'll add it to *OPEN*.

- If, by any chance, *m* has already been explored and is a part of our *OPEN* or our *CLOSE*, we already have a path to *m* from some arbitrary node, and there is one more part that we are getting from *m* to *n*. So, we need to check which is lower: the previous cost of *m* or the current cost. So, we'll check the minimum, whatever the cost will be, and we'll update *f(m)* accordingly; if the value of *f(m)* is decreased and our *m* belongs to *CLOSE*, then we will move *m* to *OPEN*.

5. We'll keep on doing this until we do not get a failure or a success.

Let's go over this with the previous example. The following diagram shows the previous example; this time, we can see the heuristic costs of all of the nodes:

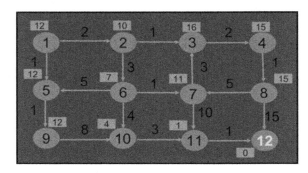

The following is an underlining assumption to the preceding algorithm:

Step 1: Initialize: *s=1*

> *OPEN{1(12)}*
> *CLOSE{}*
> *g(1)=0, h(1)=12*

> Therefore, *f(1)=12*

Step 2: If *OPEN = {}*; Terminate with Failure

> Since, *OPEN ≠ {}*; Select minimum cost successor and add it to *CLOSE{}*

> *CLOSE{1(12)}*

> *OPEN{}*

Step 3: If *1(12) ∈ G*; Terminate with Success

        Since *1(12) ∉ G*

Step 4: Expand *1(12)* to get its successor, *m*.

        We get *m = 2, 5*

        g(2)=2; h(2)=10. Therefore, *f(2)= 2+10=12*

        g(5)=1; h(5)=12. Therefore, *f(5)= 1+12=13*

        Therefore, *m=2(12) or m=5(13)*

        OPEN{2(12), 5(13)}

        Go to Step 2

        Since *OPEN ≠ {}*

        Add minimum cost successor *2(12)* to *CLOSE*

        Therefore, *CLOSE{1(12), 2(12)}*

        OPEN{5{13}}

        Since *2(12) ∉ G*

        Expand *2(12)* to get its successor, *m*.

        We get *m = 3, 6*

        g(3)=3; h(3)=16. Therefore, *f(3)= 19*

        g(6)=5; h(6)=7. Therefore, *f(6)= 12*

        Therefore, *m=3(19) or m=6(12)*

        OPEN{5(13), 3(19), 6(12)}

        Go to Step 2

        Since *OPEN ≠ {}*

        Add minimum cost successor *6(12)* to *CLOSE*

        Therefore, *CLOSE{1(12), 2(12), 6(12)}*

OPEN{5{13}, 3(19)}

Since *6(12)* ∉ *G*

Expand *6(12)* to get its successor, *m.*

We get *m = 5, 7, 10*

Since *7* ∉ *[OPEN U CLOSE]: g(7)=6; h(7)=11.* Therefore, *f(7)= 17*

Since *10* ∉ *[OPEN U CLOSE]: g(10)=9; h(10)=4.* Therefore, *f(10)= 13*

For *m=5*

Since *5* ∈ *[OPEN U CLOSE]: g(5) = min {1, 10 }= 1; f(5)=13*

OPEN{5(13), 3(19), 7(17), 10(13)}

Go to Step 2

Since *OPEN ≠ {}*

Add minimum cost successor *5(13)* to *CLOSE* (Since *5(13)* was added before *10(13)* to *OPEN*, we will consider it as the minimum cost successor)

Therefore, *CLOSE{1(12), 2(12), 6(12), 5(13)}*

OPEN{3(19), 7(17), 10(13)}

Since *5(13)* ∉ *G*

Expand *5(13)* to get its successor, *m.*

We get *m = 9*

Since *9* ∉ *[OPEN U CLOSE]: g(9)=2; h(9)=12.* Therefore, *f(9)= 14*

OPEN{5(13), 3(19), 7(17), 10(13), 9(14)}

Go to Step 2

Since *OPEN ≠ {}*

Add minimum cost successor *10(13)* to *CLOSE*

Therefore, *CLOSE{1(12), 2(12), 6(12), 5(13), 10(13)}*

OPEN{5(13), 3(19), 7(17), 9(14)}

Since *10(13) ∉ G*

Expand *10(13)* to get its successor, *m.*

We get *m = 11*

Since *11 ∉ [OPEN U CLOSE]: g(11)=2+3+4+3=12; h(11)=1.* Therefore, *f(11)= 13*

OPEN{3(19), 7(17), 9(14), 11(13)}

Go to Step 2

Since *OPEN ≠ {}*

Add minimum cost successor *11(13)* to *CLOSE*

Therefore, *CLOSE{1(12), 2(12), 6(12), 5(13), 10(13), 11(13)}*

OPEN{3(19), 7(17), 9(14)}

Since *11(13) ∉ G*

Expand *11(13)* to get its successor, *m.*

We get *m = 12*

Since *12 ∉ [OPEN U CLOSE]: g(12)=13; h(12)=0.* Therefore, *f(12)= 13*

OPEN{3(19), 7(17), 9(14), 12(13)}

Go to Step 2

Since *OPEN ≠ {}*

Add minimum cost successor *12(13)* to *CLOSE*

Therefore, *CLOSE{1(12), 2(12), 6(12), 5(13), 10(13), 11(13), 12(13)}*

OPEN{3(19), 7(17), 9(14)}

Since *12(13) ∈ G*

Therefore, we have reached the goal node, which is *12.*

Implementing an A* algorithm

We will now look at how to implement an A* algorithm. Let's start with the code. We will use the same code that we used in the Dijkstra's search algorithm. The `Vertex.java` file is as follows:

```java
public class Vertex {
    final private String id;
    final private String name;

    public Vertex(String id, String name) {
        this.id = id;
        this.name = name;
    }
// public String getId() {
// return id;
// }
//
// public String getName() {
// return name;
// }

    @Override
    public int hashCode() {
        final int prime = 31;
        int result = 1;
        result = prime * result + ((id == null) ? 0 : id.hashCode());
        return result;
    }

    @Override
    public boolean equals(Object obj) {
        if (this == obj)
            return true;
        if (obj == null)
            return false;
        if (getClass() != obj.getClass())
            return false;
        Vertex other = (Vertex) obj;
        if (id == null) {
            if (other.id != null)
                return false;
        } else if (!id.equals(other.id))
            return false;
        return true;
    }
```

```
@Override
public String toString() {
    return name;
}
```

In the `Edge.java` file, we are making one change by adding a heuristic variable, `hval`; our constructor will take that value. Aside from that, there are no changes to the following code:

```
public class Edge {
    private final String id;
    private final Vertex source;
    private final Vertex destination;
    private final int weight;
    private final int hval;

    public Edge(String id, Vertex source, Vertex destination, int weight,
int hval) {
        this.id = id;
        this.source = source;
        this.destination = destination;
        this.weight = weight;
        this.hval = hval;
    }

    public String getId() {
        return id;
    }
    public Vertex getDestination() {
        return destination;
    }

    public Vertex getSource() {
        return source;
    }
    public int getWeight() {
        return weight+hval;
    }

    //@Override
    public String toString() {
        return source + " " + destination;
    }
```

We then have the `Graph.java` file, which will have no changes, except for the previously mentioned heuristic value:

```java
import java.util.List;
public class Graph {
    private final List<Vertex> vertexes;
    private final List<Edge> edges;

    public Graph(List<Vertex> vertexes, List<Edge> edges) {
        this.vertexes = vertexes;
        this.edges = edges;
    }

    public List<Vertex> getVertexes() {
        return vertexes;
    }

    public List<Edge> getEdges() {
        return edges;
    }
}
```

Our `astr.java` file also won't have any changes. It will just calculate the minimum distance, because the minimum distance is being calculated by the actual cost. Then, we have a `Test.java` file, as follows:

```java
import java.util.ArrayList;
import java.util.LinkedList;
import java.util.List;

import static org.junit.Assert.assertNotNull;
import static org.junit.Assert.assertTrue;

public class Test {

    private List<Vertex> nodes;
    private List<Edge> edges;

    public void testExcute() {
        nodes = new ArrayList<Vertex>();
        edges = new ArrayList<Edge>();
        for (int i = 0; i < 12; i++) {
            Vertex location = new Vertex("Node_" + i, "Node_" + i);
            nodes.add(location);
        }

        addLane("Edge_0", 0, 1, 2, 12);
        addLane("Edge_1", 0, 4, 1, 12);
        addLane("Edge_2", 1, 2, 1, 16);
```

```
        addLane("Edge_3", 1, 5, 3, 7);
        addLane("Edge_4", 2, 3, 2, 14);
        addLane("Edge_5", 3, 7, 1, 15);
        addLane("Edge_6", 4, 8, 1, 12);
        addLane("Edge_7", 5, 4, 5, 12);
        addLane("Edge_8", 5, 6, 1, 11);
        addLane("Edge_9", 5, 9, 4, 4);
        addLane("Edge_10", 6, 2, 3, 16);
        addLane("Edge_11", 6, 10, 10, 1);
        addLane("Edge_12", 7, 11, 15, 0);
        addLane("Edge_13", 8, 9, 8, 4);
        addLane("Edge_14", 9, 10, 3, 1);
        addLane("Edge_15", 10, 11, 1, 0);
        addLane("Edge_16", 7, 6, 5, 11);
        // Lets check from location Loc_1 to Loc_10
        Graph graph = new Graph(nodes, edges);
        astr ast = new astr(graph);
        ast.execute(nodes.get(0));
        LinkedList<Vertex> path = ast.getPath(nodes.get(10));

        assertNotNull(path);
        assertTrue(path.size() > 0);

        for (Vertex vertex : path) {
            System.out.println(vertex);
        }

    }

    private void addLane(String laneId, int sourceLocNo, int destLocNo,
            int cost, int hval) {
        Edge lane = new Edge(laneId,nodes.get(sourceLocNo),
    nodes.get(destLocNo), cost, hval );
        edges.add(lane);
    }
```

Now, we'll assign some values to test. This time, we'll create the constructor. Also, we'll have to take our junit.jar and hamcrest-core-1.3.jar files; so, we'll import them, and in the edges, we'll assign four values instead of three. We'll have a source node, a target node (destination), the actual cost, and the heuristic value.

Run the code, and you will see the following output:

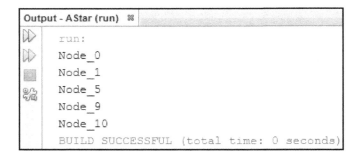

Notice that this time, we have generated a lower number of nodes, which means that we have performed the search in a more optimized fashion.

Summary

In this chapter, you learned about heuristics, and you also learned how uniform cost and A* algorithms work.

In the next chapter, you'll learn how game playing works (in other words, how AI games work). We'll cover the rule-based system and how it works in Java.

3
AI Games and the Rule-Based System

In this chapter, we will cover the following topics:

- How AI games work
- An introduction to game playing
- Implementing a rule-based system
- How to interface with Prolog in Java

Let's begin.

Introducing the min-max algorithm

In order to understand the min-max algorithm, you should get familiar with game playing and game trees. Game playing can be classified as game trees. What is a game tree? A tree is made of a **root** node, and a root node has child nodes; each child node is subdivided into multiple children.

This forms a tree, and the terminal nodes are termed **leaves**, as shown in the following diagram:

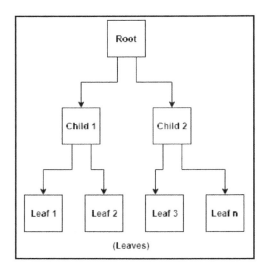

In game play, our main goal is to win the game; in other words, we try to find the best possible solution by looking ahead in the game tree. The most important thing to note about playing a game is that we don't actually go down to a particular node (or down to a complete tree), and we don't play the entire game. We are at the root position, and we are looking for the best option that is available to us, in order to maximize our chances of winning the game.

Since we are performing game playing, we will take turns, just like in a game of chess or tic-tac-toe; we take a turn, and then our opponent takes a turn. This means that all of our children, or the children of a particular node, will be our opponent's move. Our opponent's objective will be to make us lose, because whatever the game tree that we are going to develop would be in our perspective. Therefore, from our perspective, on any particular move, our objective is to win the game; once our move is done, it will be our opponent's move. The opponent's move, in our perspective, will be to make us lose. Therefore, when looking ahead, we simply search the game tree.

Consider a tree with the following types of nodes:

- **min nodes**: These are our opponent's nodes
- **max nodes**: These are our nodes

In **min** nodes, we select the minimum cost successor. Out of all of the successors that we have for a particular node, we choose the minimum. In a **max** node, we try to find out the maximum successor, because the nodes are our moves.

Now, we are not actually moving to a particular point; we are only looking ahead, performing certain computations in the memory, and trying to find the best move possible. The terminal nodes are the winning or losing nodes, but it is often not feasible to search the terminal nodes; so, we apply heuristics to compare the non-terminal nodes. The following diagram illustrates our game tree:

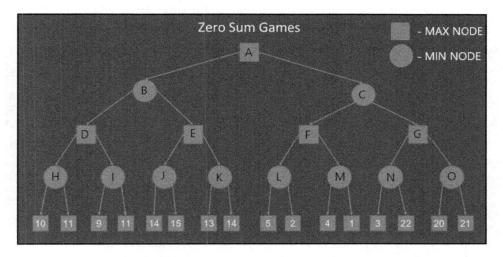

We'll start at the root node, **A**. We have two options: either the right subtree or the left subtree. If we select either of the subtrees at random, our chances of losing the game become higher. To avoid this, we will apply certain heuristics, so that our chances of winning the game will increase. Therefore, we'll try to model the game. Suppose we select **B**; our opponent will have the option to select either **D** or **E**. If our opponent selects **D**, we'll have the option to select either **H** or **I**. If our opponent chooses **H**, we will have the option to select either **10** or **11**, this is the maximum that can be performed. Our computer system does not have the RAM to process any further; therefore, from this point, we'll apply heuristics.

In the preceding diagram, the heuristic values of all of the terminal nodes can be seen. The game is not ending, and we are only looking ahead. The heuristic values comprise the maximum depth that we can go for a look ahead; after them, we will apply heuristics. The chances of winning the game at particular points are, let's say, 10%, 11%, 9%, and so on. These are the terminal values that we have.

Now, suppose that our opponent selects the **H** node. This is a min node, and a min node will always choose a minimum out of its successors. Therefore, the min node will always choose **10**, if choosing between **10** and **11**. If we move ahead, we have **9** and **11**; so, our opponent will select **9**. Similarly, our opponent will select the rest of the nodes.

Now, it's our move. **D**, **E**, **F**, and **G** are the max nodes. The max nodes will always choose the maximum value out of their successors. Therefore, we will choose **10**, **14**, **2**, and **20** as our nodes. Now it's our opponent's move again, and our opponent will always choose the minimum among his successors. This time, he will select **10** and **2**. Finally, it is our turn, and we have a max node. We will choose the maximum value successor: **10**. This is illustrated in the following diagram:

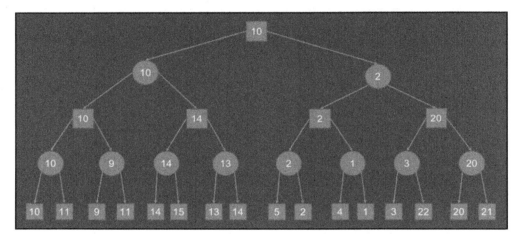

So, this is how game play works.

Implementing an example min-max algorithm

In this section, we will be implementing a min-max algorithm (a tic-tac-toe example). So, let's get to NetBeans. We will have an `ArrayList`, and we will apply randomization and take input. The following are the four classes that we'll be working with:

```
import java.util.ArrayList;
import java.util.List;
import java.util.Random;
import java.util.Scanner;
```

Then, we have to define the x and y points. In a tic-tac-toe game, there are nine tiles, and, on a one-on-one basis with the opponent, the squares are filled, as shown here:

```
class Point {

    int x, y;

    public Point(int x, int y) {
        this.x = x;
        this.y = y;
    }

    @Override
    public String toString() {
        return "[" + x + ", " + y + "]";
    }
}

class PointAndScore {

    int score;
    Point point;

    PointAndScore(int score, Point point) {
        this.score = score;
        this.point = point;
    }
}
```

So, we'll define Point, and the x and y points. This will give us the x and y values, onto which we have to enter the values. String will return us those values. PointAndScore will provide the point value and its score at each particular square, whether it is filled in or not.

The Board class will define the entire nine tiles and will take input; this will give us three states. Either X has won, or the person who has an X has won, or the person who has a 0 has won, and the available states, if the available states are Empty:

```
class Board {

    List<Point> availablePoints;
    Scanner scan = new Scanner(System.in);
    int[][] board = new int[3][3];

    public Board() {
    }
```

```
public boolean isGameOver() {
    return (hasXWon() || hasOWon() || getAvailableStates().isEmpty());
}

public boolean hasXWon() {
    if ((board[0][0] == board[1][1] && board[0][0] == board[2][2] &&
board[0][0] == 1) || (board[0][2] == board[1][1] && board[0][2] ==
board[2][0] && board[0][2] == 1)) {
        return true;
    }
    for (int i = 0; i < 3; ++i) {
        if (((board[i][0] == board[i][1] && board[i][0] == board[i][2]
&& board[i][0] == 1)
                || (board[0][i] == board[1][i] && board[0][i] ==
board[2][i] && board[0][i] == 1))) {
            return true;
        }
    }
    return false;
}


public boolean hasOWon() {
    if ((board[0][0] == board[1][1] && board[0][0] == board[2][2] &&
board[0][0] == 2) || (board[0][2] == board[1][1] && board[0][2] ==
board[2][0] && board[0][2] == 2)) {
        return true;
    }
    for (int i = 0; i < 3; ++i) {
        if ((board[i][0] == board[i][1] && board[i][0] == board[i][2]
&& board[i][0] == 2)
                || (board[0][i] == board[1][i] && board[0][i] ==
board[2][i] && board[0][i] == 2)) {
            return true;
        }
    }

    return false;
}

public List<Point> getAvailableStates() {
    availablePoints = new ArrayList<>();
    for (int i = 0; i < 3; ++i) {
        for (int j = 0; j < 3; ++j) {
            if (board[i][j] == 0) {
                availablePoints.add(new Point(i, j));
            }
        }
    }
```

```
            return availablePoints;
    }

    public void placeAMove(Point point, int player) {
        board[point.x][point.y] = player; //player = 1 for X, 2 for O
    }
    void takeHumanInput() {
        System.out.println("Your move: ");
        int x = scan.nextInt();
        int y = scan.nextInt();
        Point point = new Point(x, y);
        placeAMove(point, 2);
    }

    public void displayBoard() {
        System.out.println();

        for (int i = 0; i < 3; ++i) {
            for (int j = 0; j < 3; ++j) {
                System.out.print(board[i][j] + " ");
            }
            System.out.println();

        }
    }
    Point computersMove;
    public int minimax(int depth, int turn) {
        if (hasXWon()) return +1;
        if (hasOWon()) return -1;

        List<Point> pointsAvailable = getAvailableStates();
        if (pointsAvailable.isEmpty()) return 0;

        int min = Integer.MAX_VALUE, max = Integer.MIN_VALUE;
        for (int i = 0; i < pointsAvailable.size(); ++i) {
            Point point = pointsAvailable.get(i);
            if (turn == 1) {
                placeAMove(point, 1);
                int currentScore = minimax(depth + 1, 2);
                max = Math.max(currentScore, max);
                if(depth == 0)System.out.println("Score for position
"+(i+1)+" = "+currentScore);
                if(currentScore >= 0){ if(depth == 0) computersMove =
point;}
                if(currentScore == 1){board[point.x][point.y] = 0; break;}
                if(i == pointsAvailable.size()-1 && max < 0){if(depth ==
0)computersMove = point;}
            } else if (turn == 2) {
```

```
                    placeAMove(point, 2);
                    int currentScore = minimax(depth + 1, 1);
                    min = Math.min(currentScore, min);
                    if(min == -1){board[point.x][point.y] = 0; break;}
                }
                board[point.x][point.y] = 0; //Reset this point
            }
        return turn == 1?max:min;
    }
}
```

If X has won, we have to check which values are equal, such as board `[0]` `[0]` is equal to `[1]` `[1]` and `[0]` `[0]` is equal to `[2]` `[2]`. This means that the diagonals are equal, or `[0]` `[0]` is equal to 1, or board 0 is equal to `[1]` `[1]`. Either we have all of the diagonals, or we have any one of the horizontal lines, or we have all three squares in a vertical line. If this happens, we will return `true`; otherwise, we'll check the other values on the board. The following part of the code will check the values, and will return `false` if they do not comply with the preceding conditions:

```
    public boolean hasXWon() {
        if ((board[0][0] == board[1][1] && board[0][0] == board[2][2] &&
board[0][0] == 1) || (board[0][2] == board[1][1] && board[0][2] ==
board[2][0] && board[0][2] == 1)) {
            return true;
        }
        for (int i = 0; i < 3; ++i) {
            if (((board[i][0] == board[i][1] && board[i][0] == board[i][2] &&
board[i][0] == 1)
                        || (board[0][i] == board[1][i] && board[0][i] ==
board[2][i] && board[0][i] == 1))) {
                return true;
            }
        }
        return false;
    }
```

Next, we will see whether 0 has won; so, we will do the same thing for 0. Here, we will check whether the value is 2. Then, if nobody has won, we'll check the available states for the users, and we'll print them. We will then have `placeAMove`, and either player 1 will move or player 2 will move.

Next, we have `takeHumanInput`; so, we'll take the human input for the x and y points, and we will display the board using the `displayBoard` method; finally, we'll apply a min-max algorithm. So, we'll check if X has won or if 0 has won; if not, we'll start playing the game, and we will print the score positions. Finally, in the `main` class, we'll start with who will make the first move (either the computer or the user). If our user starts a move, we have to provide the values in x and y coordinates (in an x and y plane); otherwise, the computer will start the move, and every time, we will have to check whether X has won. If X has won, we will print `Unfortunately, you lost!` if 0 has won, we will print `You won!` if both win, then we will print `It's a draw!`

Run the program to get the following output:

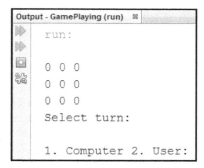

The preceding output is the initial position of the port. This has been printed at the initial point. Now, we have to select our turn. Suppose that we enter 1; we will get the following output:

```
1. Computer 2. User:
1

1 0 0
0 0 0
0 0 0
Your move:
```

The computer's turn was first, and the computer placed the position at [0] [0]. Now, it's our move; so, we place [0] [2]. This will enter 2 in the last position on our board, as shown in the following screenshot:

```
Your move:
0 2

1 0 2
0 0 0
0 0 0
Score for position 1 = -1
Score for position 2 = 1

1 0 2
1 0 0
0 0 0
Your move:
```

Our 2 has been placed at [0] [2]. The preceding screenshot shows our current positions. The computer has placed a mark on [1] [0]. Let's place a mark on [2] [0], as follows:

```
Your move:
2 0

1 0 2
1 0 0
2 0 0
Score for position 1 = -1
Score for position 2 = 1

1 0 2
1 1 0
2 0 0
Your move:
```

We now have a position over `[2]` `[0]` and have blocked the computer. Now, the computer has entered 1 at `[1]` `[1]`. Let's put a mark on `[1]` `[2]`, and block the computer again:

```
Your move:
1 2

1 0 2
1 1 2
2 0 0
Score for position 1 = -1
Score for position 2 = -1
Score for position 3 = 1

1 0 2
1 1 2
2 0 1
Unfortunately, you lost!
BUILD SUCCESSFUL (total time: 56 seconds)
```

The computer has entered 1 at `[2]` `[2]`, and has won the game.

Installing Prolog

We will now show you how to install Prolog onto your system. In your browser, go to `http://www.swi-prolog.org/download/stable`:

	24,613,399 bytes	SWI-Prolog **7.6.4** for Microsoft Windows (64 bit) Self-installing executable for Microsoft's Windows 64-bit editions. Requires at least Windows 7. See the reference manual for deciding on whether to use the 32- or 64-bits version. This binary is linked against GMP 6.1.1 which is covered by the LGPL license. **SHA256**: ad0a3768f039997573a39b60beb3bff3ce86810982c53b6d14e7a83613406ea9
	23,350,009 bytes	SWI-Prolog **7.6.4** for Microsoft Windows (32 bit) Self-installing executable for MS-Windows. Requires at least Windows 7. Installs **swipl-win.exe** and **swipl.exe**. This binary is linked against GMP 6.1.1 which is covered by the LGPL license. **SHA256**: 756834f8a26ad40f95af3c05cd09205664d027d04e12bda767e5459325c999ed
	23,848,243 bytes	SWI-Prolog **7.6.4** for MacOSX 10.6 (Snow Leopard) and later on **intel** Mac OS X disk image with **relocatable application bundle**. Needs xquartz (X11) installed for running the development tools. Currently, version 2.7.11 is required. You can check the version by opening an X11 application and then checking `about' in the X11 menu. The bundle also provides the commandline tools in `Contents/MacOS`. The command line tools need at least MacOS **10.6** (Snow Leopard). The graphical application needs at least MacOS **10.7** (Lion). **SHA256**: d318f9c19c9bc86dd5e37392bc44bdfd7080d209cf9f7b01dd51b353665b6dc6

If you are using the Windows OS, you can download a 64-bit version or a 32-bit version, based on your Windows version. If you have Mac OS, then you can download the Mac version. You can install it as follows:

- For Windows, you have to download the .exe file and run it. Continue with the installation process by clicking on **Next,** and you will be able to get Prolog onto your system.
- For Mac, you have to download the .dmg file and extract it onto your system. Then, copy it into your applications, and install it.
- SWI-Prolog comes with Linux by default, so on Linux, you do not have to install it.

An introduction to rule-based systems with Prolog

Now, we'll look at how to create a knowledge base and apply inference in Prolog. Let's start by looking at the Prolog environment:

- If you are on Windows, go to **Programs | Prolog**
- If you are on a Mac, go to **Applications | Prolog**
- In Linux, go to the Terminal and type Prolog, and the environment will come up

The following screenshot shows the Prolog environment in Windows:

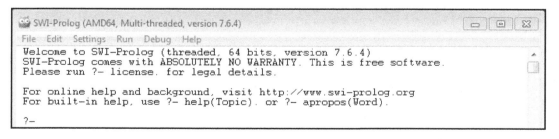

The `?-` object is the Prolog prompt, or the Prolog interpreter. Whatever we type here will be executed; Prolog will be treated as a predicate, and it will give the result as either `true` or `false`. Therefore, if we want to create new rules, we go to **File** and either create a new knowledge base (using **New ...**) or **Edit ...** an existing knowledge base, as follows:

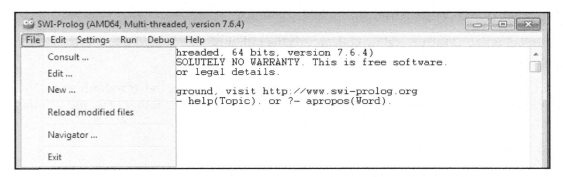

If you're working on Windows or Mac, you will have to open your knowledge base in a text editor. You can use gedit, you can use Mino on Linux, or you can use the text editor that is available with Mac. We've already created a knowledge base, so we won't be writing the rules; we'll just be demonstrating them. The following screenshot shows our knowledge base:

Suppose that Michael is the child of Vito; we'll create a predicate with the name `child`, and pass two terms to it: one is `michael`, and the is `vito`. Then, suppose that `sonny` is the child of `vito`, and `fredo` is the child of `vito`. We will create two more facts, as follows:

- `child(anthony, michael).`: Anthony is the child of Michael.
- `child(mary, michael).`: Mary is the child of Michael.

So, if somebody is the child of somebody, then that somebody is the father of that somebody: X is the father of Y. In Prolog, the conditional part works in a reverse manner. The `father(X, Y)` object is the consequent that we need, and `child(Y, Z)` is the antecedent for it. Then, if Y is the child of X, X is the father of Y:

```
father(X, Y) :- child(Y, X).
```

In Prolog, we read the preceding code as X is the father of Y, provided that Y is the child of X, and we use a full stop as a statement terminator.

Similarly, we are creating a new rule: `grandfather(X, Y)`. X is the grandfather of Y, provided that Y is the child of Z and X is the father of Z. If X is the father of Z, and Y is the child of Z, then we have an X and Y relationship.

Let's compile this by navigating to **Compile** | **Make**:

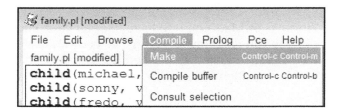

After it is compiled, we will try to open the knowledge base in Prolog. To do so, we need to know the path where the knowledge base is stored. Then, go to Prolog and use the following command on the path:

```
?- consult('C:/Users/admin/Documents/Prolog/family.pl').
```

Notice that we have to replace the backslashes with forward slashes.

Now, we can ask questions of the knowledge base, such as the following:

```
child(soony, vito).
```

The knowledge base will respond with either `true` or `false`:

```
?- child(soony,vito).
false.
```

It has returned `false`, which means that we don't know the names of the children of `vito`. To find the children of `vito`, we use `X`, as follows:

```
?- child(X, vito).
```

 The uppercase character (`X`) will be treated as a variable, whereas a lowercase character (a word starting with a lowercase letter, such as `vito`) is considered a constant.

We get the following result:

```
?- child(X, vito).
X = michael ;
X = sonny ;
X = fredo.
```

Now, let's ask again, with the following command:

```
?- child(sonny,vito).
```

We get the following output:

```
?- child(sonny,vito).
true .
```

Previously, the response was `false`, because we provided the wrong spelling of `sonny`. This means that the spelling should match.

Similarly, we can ask for the `father` with the following command:

```
?- father(vito, sonny)
```

We get the following output:

```
?- father(vito, sonny).
true .
```

We get `true`, which means that `vito` is the `father` of `sonny`. We can find the children of `michael` by typing the following command:

```
?- father(michael, X).
```

We get the following output:

```
?- father(michael, X).
X = anthony ;
X = mary.
```

We get that `anthony` is the son of `michael`, and `mary` is the daughter of `michael`, which means that `michael` is the father of `anthony` and `mary`.

Similarly, we can ask for the grandfather, as follows:

```
?- grandfather(vito, X).
```

We get that `vito` is the `grandfather` of `anthony` and `mary`:

```
?- grandfather(vito, X).
X = anthony ;
X = mary .
```

As you can see, we have not created the facts for `father` and `grandfather`, but they have been inferred by a Prolog interpreter, and we are able to get answers to questions, based on the predicates `father` and `grandfather`.

That is how we can write rules and facts into our knowledge base, and ask questions with Prolog. If we want to see all of the father and son relationships, we can ask the following:

```
?- father(X, Y).
```

We will get all of the father and son pairs, as follows:

```
?- father(X, Y).
X = vito,
Y = michael ;
X = vito,
Y = sonny ;
X = vito,
Y = fredo ;
X = michael,
Y = anthony ;
X = michael,
Y = mary.
```

We get that `vito` is the father of `michael`, `vito` is the father of `sonny`, and so on.

Similarly, we can use the `grandfather` relationship, as follows:

```
?- grandfather(X, Y).
```

We get that `vito` is the grandfather of `anthony`, and `vito` is the grandfather of `mary`:

```
?- grandfather(X, Y).
X = vito,
Y = anthony ;
X = vito,
Y = mary.
```

Setting up Prolog with Java

Now, you will see how to download a JPL library, and how to interface with Prolog using `JPL` in Java.

In your browser, go to `http://www.java2s.com/Code/Jar/j/Downloadjpljar.htm`:

```
jpl/jpl.jar.zip( 27 k)
```

The download jar file contains the following class files or Java source files.

```
META-INF/MANIFEST.MF
jpl.Atom.class
jpl.Compound.class
```

This is one of the popular repositories of all of the known JAR files that have been created, and it preserves all of those JAR files. We will get all of the information and all of the classes that are available in this `JPL` library, and we'll use them in our code. Click on **jpl/jpl.jar.zip(27 k)** to download the library. Then, you will have to extract it to get the `jpl.jar` file.

Once we have extracted our JAR file, we can check the code to see if it is working. Therefore, we will go to NetBeans. In NetBeans, we'll go to our project, right-click on it, and go to the **Properties** option. In **Properties**, we'll go to **Libraries** and the **Add JAR/Folder** option:

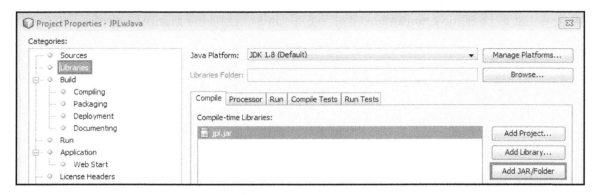

In **Add JAR/Folder**, we have to provide the path where we have extracted our `jpl.jar` file. Once we have selected the path, we will click on **Open**:

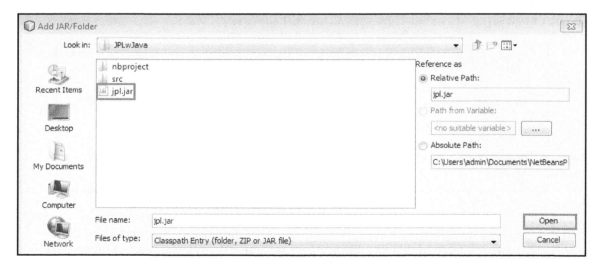

We will import this file into our Java code, as follows:

```
import jpl.*;

public class JPLwJava {

    /**
     * @param args the command line arguments
     */
    public static void main(String[] args) {
        // TODO code application logic here
        System.out.println("Hello Prolog");
    }
}
```

The `import jpl.*;` command imports the JPL library into our code. For now, we'll simply print `Hello Prolog`.

Run the code to get the following output:

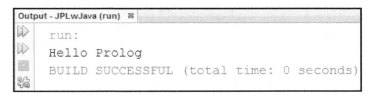

The `Hello Prolog` message means that our JPL library has been incorporated into our code, so we can do interfacing between Prolog and Java.

Executing Prolog queries using Java

Now, we'll look at how to ask Prolog queries in Java. Let's get to the Java code and see how this can be done.

Create a Java project in NetBeans, and type the following code:

```
import java.util.Map;
import jpl.Query;
import jpl.JPL;

public class ProrlogJava {

    /**
     * @param args the command line arguments
```

```
        */
    public static void main(String[] args) {
        // TODO code application logic here
        String t1 =
"consult('/Users/admin/Documents/NetBeansProjects/JPLwJava/family.pl')";
        System.out.println(t1 + " " + (Query.hasSolution(t1) ? "succeeded"
: "failed"));
        String t2 = "child(sonny, vito)";
        System.out.println(t2 + " " + (Query.hasSolution(t2) ? "provable" :
"not provable"));
        String t3 = "grandfather(vito, anthony)";
        System.out.println(t3 + " " + (Query.hasSolution(t3) ? "provable" :
"not provable"));
    }
}
```

First, we have to call the JPL libraries by adding the jpl.jar file, as seen in the previous section. Once we have them, we'll import two classes from the JPL package: the jpl.Query class and the jpl.JPL class.

Next, we have to provide a String, where we will type consult and the name of our file.

The Prolog files are saved in a .pl format, or a text format.

Then, we can call Query.hasSolution(t1). If our knowledge base opens in Prolog, we'll get a succeeded message; otherwise, we'll get a failed message. This is a simple conditional operator.

Next, we will query: child(sonny, vito). This will give us either provable or not provable. If it is true, a message will be returned that it is provable; otherwise, we will get the message not provable. Similarly, we can ask: grandfather(vito, anthony). If this is provable, we'll get provable; otherwise, we'll get not provable.

Let's run this and see what happens, as follows:

```
Output - ProrlogJava (run)  ⊗
run:
consult('family.pl') succeeded
child(sonny, vito) provable
grandfather(vito, anthony) provable
BUILD SUCCESSFUL (total time: 0 seconds)
```

We consulted our database, and `family.pl` was successfully loaded into the memory. Then, we asked the question of whether `sonny` is the `child` of `vito`, and the response was `provable`; similarly, we asked whether `vito` is the `grandfather` of `anthony`, and it was `provable`. That is how we can use Prolog in Java.

Summary

In this chapter, you learned how game play works, how you can implement tic-tac-toe in Java, how to install Prolog, how to download a `JPL` library, and how to interface with Prolog in Java.

In the next chapter, we'll cover interfacing with Weka.

Interfacing with Weka

4

In this chapter, we will be working with datasets. The general format of a dataset is a **comma-separated value (CSV)** file, and Weka works with a special kind of format, known as an **Attribute-Relation File Format (ARFF)** file. We will look at how to convert a CSV file to an ARFF file, and vice versa.

In this chapter, we will cover the following topics:

- A brief introduction to Weka
- Installing and interfacing with Weka
- Reading and writing datasets
- Converting datasets

First, let's look at an introduction to Weka.

An introduction to Weka

Weka is a suite of machine learning software written in Java. It was developed by the University of Waikato, New Zealand. It is a free software, available under the GNU **General Public License (GPL)**, and the algorithms can be either applied directly to a dataset or called from our own Java code.

When we download Weka and start using it, it provides us with its own GUI. We can use the GUI to work with our own datasets. If we want to enhance the capabilities of Weka, we should use it in our Java code. The official website for Weka is located at `https://www.cs.waikato.ac.nz/ml/weka/`. It is on Waikato University's official website. Its current version is 3. We can find all of the information about Weka on its website. We will find various sections, such as **Getting started**, **Further information**, and **Developers**.

In **Getting started**, the following options are available:

- **Requirements**: The requirements for using Weka.
- **Download**: On the **Download** page, we can go to the **Snapshot** section, where we can download Weka.
- **Documentation**: If we go to the **Documentation** page, it will provide us with a lot of the documentation available for Weka. There is also the Weka Wiki, where we can get most of the information that we will need, a list of packages, and some videos.
- **FAQ**: This is comprised of frequently asked questions.
- **Getting Help**: This provides further assistance, if needed.

The **Project** page provides the machine learning group. It's Waikato's Department of Computer Science machine learning group, which developed the software. We can also read about their basic objectives for the development of Weka.

Installing and interfacing with Weka

We will now learn how to download Weka. In order to download Weka, go to the download website at `https://www.cs.waikato.ac.nz/ml/weka/downloading.html`. Upon visiting the page, we will be provided with information about downloads. If we scroll down, we will get information about the stable versions; depending on the machine that we have, we can download the version of Weka that we want, with the following options:

- For Windows, the file will be an EXE file; we just need to click on it, and it will be available in our programs.
- For Mac, it will be a DMG file; we will have to extract it and paste it into our applications.
- For Linux, upon extraction of the TAR file, we will get all of the packages that are required for running Weka, and we can run it with a `weka.jar` file by using the `java -jar weka.jar` command.

We can run the downloaded file on our system, and follow the instructions to install Weka. Once it has installed, open it, and we will see the following interface:

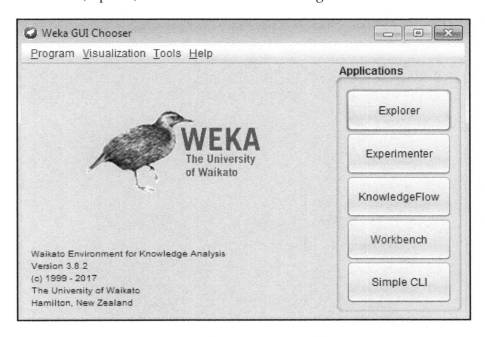

The preceding screenshot shows the Weka GUI. We can see the **Program** option, **Visualization**, and **Tools**. In **Tools**, we will see the **Package manager**, where we can install any package that is available on Weka:

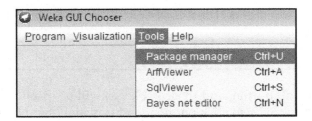

There is a very big list of package managers that are available, as shown in the following screenshot:

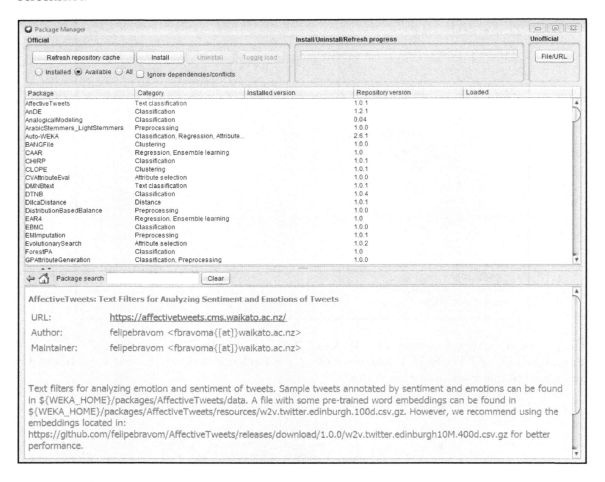

We can click on the **Install** button, and those packages will be installed. If we have already installed certain packages, we can click on them and uninstall them by clicking on the **Uninstall** button. That is how we can install and uninstall the packages.

We will now go to the Weka Explorer. Click on the **Explorer** button under **Applications**, and we will see a new window, as shown in the following screenshot:

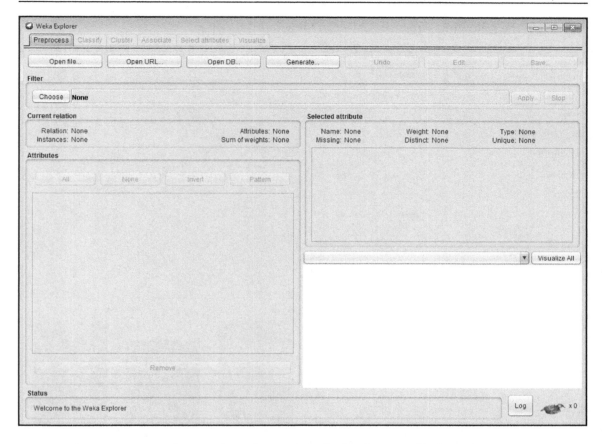

First, we have to open a dataset, in order to classify the dataset. Click on the **Open file...** button. In the `Weka` folder, we will see a `data` folder. The `data` folder will have the datasets that are available:

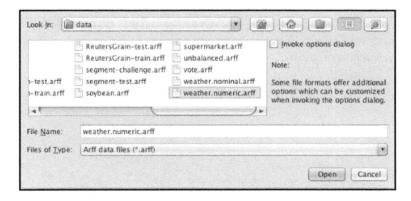

As seen in the following screenshot, we can view our dataset:

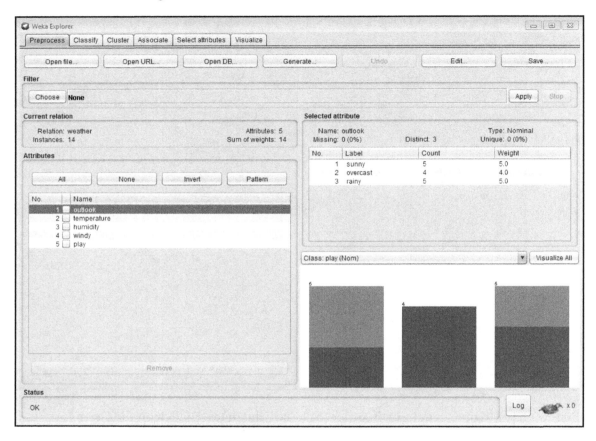

The preceding dataset has five attributes. The first attribute is outlook, and outlook has three labels with three distinct values under the Label column: sunny, with a Count of 5; overcast, with a Count of 4; and rainy, with a Count of 5. Similarly, there is the windy attribute, and windy has two kinds of values, TRUE and FALSE, with counts, as seen in the following screenshot:

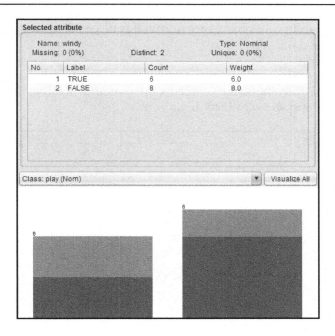

The `play` attribute has two distinct values, `yes` and `no`, along with their counts, as shown in the following screenshot:

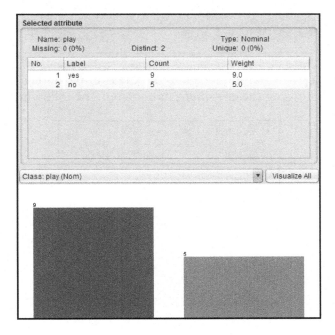

The `outlook`, `windy`, and `play` objects are nominal types of data, and `temperature` and `humidity` are numeric data.

The `temperature` attribute has 12 values, since it is a numeric value, and we can get some numerical information from the values, such as the maximum value, the minimum value, the mean of the value, and the standard deviation:

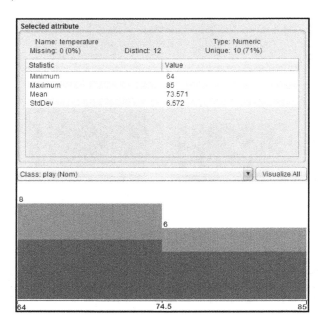

If we want to classify a particular model, go to the **Classify** tab and click on **Choose**; we will get the option of choosing the classifiers, as shown in the following screenshot:

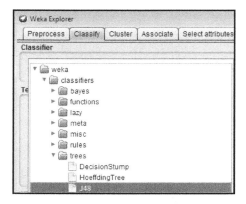

Click on the `trees` folder. Suppose that we want to perform a J48 classification: click on **J48** option and click on the **Start** button. A J48 classifier will be built using a 10-fold classification, and the statistics for that particular data will be displayed, as shown in the following screenshot:

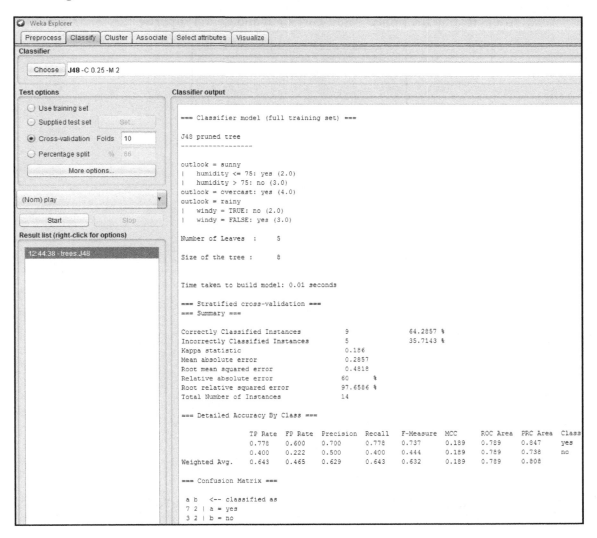

Calling the Weka environment into Java

To call a Weka environment into Java, perform the following steps:

1. Create a new project.
2. After creating the project, right-click on it and go to **Properties**:

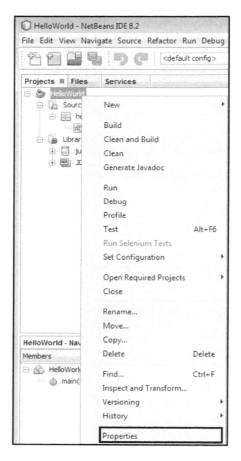

3. In the **Properties** tab, select **Libraries**, click on **Add JAR/Folder**, and give the path to the `weka.jar` file:

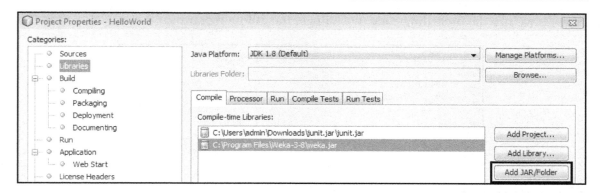

4. Once we have a path for the `weka.jar` file, we can use Weka. Replace the code in the project with the following code:

```
package helloworld;

/**
 *
 * @author admin
 */
import weka.*;
public class HelloWorld {

    /**
     * @param args the command line arguments
     */
    public static void main(String[] args) {
        // TODO code application logic here
        System.out.println("Hello World");
    }
}
```

As we can see in the preceding code, we have replaced `import juint.framework.*;` with `import weka.*;`.

Please note that the moment we write the preceding code, we will get suggestions for the Weka packages. That means that we have access to Weka in our Java environment.

Henceforth, in all of the projects, we will be using the `weka.jar` file. Therefore, every time we create a new project, we will have to `import` the `weka.jar` file in the **Libraries** window.

Now, if we run the preceding code, we will get the following output:

```
Output - HelloWorld (run) ✖
run:
Hello World
BUILD SUCCESSFUL (total time: 0 seconds)
```

Reading and writing datasets

We will now look at how to read and write a dataset. Let's get to our Java code. Create a project and name it `Datasets`. Now, import the `weka.jar` file, as performed in the previous section. Once we have the `weka.jar` file available, we can read the `core`, `Instance` interfaces, `ArffSaver`, `DataSource`, and `io.File` packages, as shown in the following screenshot:

```
import weka.core.Instances;
import weka.core.converters.ArffSaver;
import weka.core.converters.ConverterUtils.DataSource;
import java.io.File;
```

We will start with `DataSource`. `DataSource` is a class that helps us to open a dataset file that is available in Weka. By default, Weka works with ARFF files; see the following code:

```
DataSource src = new
DataSource("/Users/admin/wekafiles/data/weather.numeric.arff");
Instances dt= src.getDataSet();
System.out.println(dt.toSummaryString());
ArffSaver as = new ArffSaver();
```

As we can see in the preceding code, we created an object for `DataSource` and provided a path to the ARFF file that we need to open. This will only provide a path to an ARFF file; it will not open it. In the working memory, there is a class called `Instances`, and we have created an object, `dt`, for the `Instances` class. We'll call the `getDataSet` method with the object of `DataSource` and `src`. This will open that particular dataset into memory in the `dt` object. We can print whatever is available in that particular dataset by using the `toSummaryString` method. Once it has been read and opened, we can write it onto the hard disk by using the `ArffSaver` class. We will create an object (`as`) for it, as follows:

```
as.setInstances(dt);
```

This will only assign all of the data that is available with `dt` object to the `as` object. It will not save it, as of right now. Now, we have to give a name to the dataset; so, we will call the `setFile` method and we'll provide `weather.arff` as filename to our dataset using a `File` object:

```
as.setFile(new File("weather.arff"));
```

Now, the dataset has been given a name, but it still has not been saved in the memory. We will now call a `writeBatch` method, as follows:

```
as.writeBatch();
```

Finally, everything will get saved to the memory with the filename (`weather.arff`). When we execute the code, we will see the following output:

```
Output - Datasets (run)  %

run:
Relation Name:  weather
Num Instances:  14
Num Attributes: 5

      Name               Type  Nom  Int Real   Missing      Unique   Dist
1 outlook                Nom  100%   0%   0%    0 /  0%    0 /  0%    3
2 temperature            Num    0% 100%   0%    0 /  0%   10 / 71%   12
3 humidity               Num    0% 100%   0%    0 /  0%    7 / 50%   10
4 windy                  Nom  100%   0%   0%    0 /  0%    0 /  0%    2
5 play                   Nom  100%   0%   0%    0 /  0%    0 /  0%    2

BUILD SUCCESSFUL (total time: 0 seconds)
```

It has the `Relation Name` as `weather`, which has `14` instances and `5` attributes. It shows the statistics of the attributes. If we go to our `Datasets` project folder in NetBeans, we can check whether the `weather.arff` file has been saved:

Name	Date modified	Type	Size
build	13-08-2018 15:25	File folder	
nbproject	13-08-2018 14:56	File folder	
src	13-08-2018 14:56	File folder	
test	13-08-2018 15:01	File folder	
build.xml	13-08-2018 14:56	XML Document	4 KB
manifest.mf	13-08-2018 14:56	MF File	1 KB
weather.arff	13-08-2018 15:40	ARFF Data File	1 KB

Open the `weather.arff` file in a text editor, and we will see that the dataset has been saved in the file. The following screenshot shows what an ARFF file looks like:

```
weather.arff
1    @relation weather
2
3    @attribute outlook {sunny,overcast,rainy}
4    @attribute temperature numeric
5    @attribute humidity numeric
6    @attribute windy {TRUE,FALSE}
7    @attribute play {yes,no}
8
9    @data
10   sunny,85,85,FALSE,no
11   sunny,80,90,TRUE,no
12   overcast,83,86,FALSE,yes
13   rainy,70,96,FALSE,yes
14   rainy,68,80,FALSE,yes
15   rainy,65,70,TRUE,no
16   overcast,64,65,TRUE,yes
17   sunny,72,95,FALSE,no
18   sunny,69,70,FALSE,yes
19   rainy,75,80,FALSE,yes
20   sunny,75,70,TRUE,yes
21   overcast,72,90,TRUE,yes
22   overcast,81,75,FALSE,yes
23   rainy,71,91,TRUE,no
```

The file has a `relation`, where we can give the name of the file, and it also has an `@attribute` object. The `@attribute` object tells us that these are the attributes of the file, and, in the curly braces, we can assign categorical values. For example, the `temperature` and `humidity` attributes are `numeric` values, `windy` is a Boolean value, and `@attribute play` is a class that can have `yes` and `no`. Then, we have `@data`, where all the tuples with the attribute values are displayed. That is how an ARFF file works.

If we don't have the header data, then it is a CSV file.

Converting datasets

In this section, we will look at how to convert a dataset. We will learn how to convert a CSV file to an ARFF file, and vice versa.

Converting an ARFF file to a CSV file

First, let's look at the code. Suppose that we have a `weather.arff` file. We will first import the following packages:

```
import weka.core.Instances;
import weka.core.converters.ArffLoader;
import weka.core.converters.CSVSaver;
import java.io.File;
```

We have started with the `ArffLoader` class, and have created an object, `loader`, for it:

```
ArffLoader loader = new ArffLoader();
```

We have then assigned a filename, `weather.arff`, to the `ArffLoader` class, as seen in the following code:

```
loader.setSource(new File("weather.arff")); //Use the path where your file
is saved.
```

We have also called the `loader.setSource` method and assigned a filename to it by using our `File` object. Once this is done, we will load this particular dataset into the memory in our `Instances` object, `data`, as follows:

```
Instances data = loader.getDataSet();
```

Now, we need to create an object for our `CSVSaver` class and instantiate it:

```
CSVSaver saver = new CSVSaver();
```

Now, we need to set the instances; so, we need to provide the object for our `Instances` object to the `setInstances` method, as follows:

```
saver.setInstances(data);
```

Once we have done this, our ARFF dataset has been converted into a CSV dataset in the memory, but it has not been saved onto the disk. If we want to save it onto the disk, we have to use a `setFile` method and assign a filename using our `File` object:

```
saver.setFile(new File("weather.csv"));
```

The `File` object will be passed to the `setFile` method, and once we have done this, we have assigned a name (that is, `weather.csv`) to the dataset, but we still have not saved it onto the disk.

Upon calling the `writeBatch` method, our entire dataset will be saved onto the disk:

```
saver.writeBatch();
```

Let's try running the entire code; we should get the following output:

Now, let's go to the disk and see if the dataset has been created, as shown in the following screenshot:

We can see that a new `weather.csv` file has been created, using the `weather.arff` file. This is our CSV file, which can be opened in Notepad or Excel, as shown here:

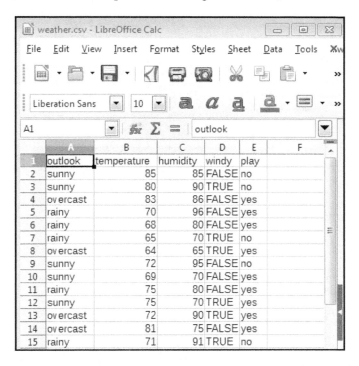

Generally, all CSV files open directly in any of the spreadsheet applications. Since CSV is a comma-separated value, all of the comma-separated values have been assigned to one particular set. Therefore, `outlook`, `temperature`, `humidity`, `windy`, and `play` have been assigned to certain cells in one particular row, and all of their values have been assigned to the corresponding columns. That is how our file is converted to a dataset. If we compare the ARFF and CSV files, we can note that the header data has been removed from the CSV file.

If we want to compare the two files, we can open both files in a text editor, as shown in the following screenshot:

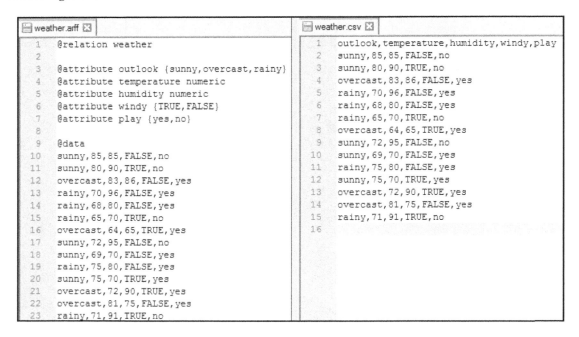

In the CSV file, we only have the header values. The attribute values from the ARFF file have been converted into the first row of the CSV file, and then, we see the values. That is how a CSV file is created.

Converting a CSV file to an ARFF file

Now, let's see if we can convert a CSV file to an ARFF file. We will do the opposite of what we did in the previous section.

First, import the following packages:

```
import weka.core.Instances;
import weka.core.converters.ArffSaver;
import weka.core.converters.CSVLoader;
import java.io.File;
```

Notice that this time, we will be importing the ArffSaver and CSVLoader classes, instead of the ArffLoader and CSVSaver classes.

This time, the very first thing that we did was create an object for the CSVLoader class and assign the CSV file to the CSVLoader class, using the setSource method of our CSVLoader object:

```
CSVLoader loader = new CSVLoader();
loader.setSource(new
File("/Users/admin/Documents/NetBeansProjects/Arff2CSV/weather.csv"));
```

Then, we opened the CSV dataset in our memory, using an Instances object:

```
Instances data = loader.getDataSet();
```

Once we have done this, we will need to save it in an ARFF format. Therefore, we have created a saver object for ArffSaver, and then, we have assigned in to Instances, the dataset that we wish to save in an ARFF file:

```
ArffSaver saver = new ArffSaver();
saver.setInstances(data);
```

Then, we used the saver object and called the setFile method to assign the name to this ArffSaver, as follows:

```
saver.setFile(new File("weather.arff"));
```

The setFile method will use the File object, and we will assign the name weather.arff to it. Now, everything has been done in the memory, the dataset has been internally converted to an ARFF format, and we have assigned a name to it (weather.arff); but, we still have not saved it onto the disk.

The writeBatch() method will save the complete dataset onto the hard disk:

```
saver.writeBatch();
```

Run the code to get the following output:

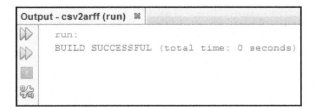

Since our build has been successful, we have our `weather.csv` being converted into `weather.arff`. Let's go to the disk and see if it worked:

In the preceding screenshot, we can see that the ARFF file has been created. We have shown how we can create an ARFF file from a CSV file. We do not need to do any manual work to assign the relations and the attributes, because they are automatically assigned by Weka if we provide our CSV file. Weka takes care of the attributes; it also takes care of what type of attribute it is. For example, `outlook` is categorical data, because it has just three types of values; so, those categories have been assigned to `outlook`. Since `temperature` takes all numeric values, it has automatically been assigned numeric by Weka, and since `humidity` also has only numeric values, it is also numeric. The `windy` object is, again, a `TRUE/FALSE` value; therefore, it is also a categorical type of data. The `play` object also has only two types of values, so it is, again, categorical data.

That is how we convert our datasets from CSV to ARFF, or ARFF to CSV.

Summary

In this chapter, we covered Weka and how to install it. We also learned how to read and write datasets, and how to convert them.

In the next chapter, we will learn how to handle attributes.

5
Handling Attributes

In this chapter, you will learn how to filter attributes, how to discretize attributes, and how to perform attribute selection. When we filter attributes, we will want to remove certain attributes from our datasets. To do so, we will use a `Remove` class from an unsupervised `filters` package, along with an attribute called `-R`. In this chapter, we will also use discretization and binning.

We will cover the following topics in this chapter:

- Filtering attributes
- Discretizing attributes
- Attribute selection

Let's begin!

Filtering attributes

We will learn how to filter attributes in this section. Let's start with the code.

We will first import the following packages and classes:

```
import weka.core.Instances;
import weka.core.converters.ArffSaver;
import java.io.File;
import weka.core.converters.ConverterUtils.DataSource;
import weka.filters.Filter;
import weka.filters.unsupervised.attribute.Remove;
```

We imported the `Instances`, `ArffSaver`, `File`, and `DataSource` classes from their respective packages, as seen in the preceding code. We used them in the previous chapter, as well. The `Instance` class will take the database into the memory, and we will work with the dataset in the memory. The `ArffSaver` class will help us to save our dataset onto the disk. The `File` class will give the name to the disk, and the `DataSource` class will open the dataset from the disk.

As you can see in the preceding code snippet, we imported a new class, `Filter`, from the `weka.filters` package. We can apply filters using the `Filter` class. The filter that we will apply will be an unsupervised filter from the `unsupervised.attribute` package.

We will first take the ARFF file into our `DataSource` object; then, we will store it in the memory by using an `Instances` class `dt` object, as follows:

```
DataSource src = new DataSource("weather.arff");//path to the ARFF file on
your system.
Instances dt = src.getDataSet();
```

We have created a `String` object, where we can put all of the options that we want to use for filtering our attribute. Since we want to remove one attribute, we'll use `-R`, and we'll include the number of the attribute that we wish to delete:

```
String[] op =  new String[]{"-R","2"};
```

We will then create an object for the `Remove` class and set the options for the `Remove` class using our `String` object, as follows:

```
Remove rmv = new Remove();
rmv.setOptions(op);
```

We will also put the `setInputFormat` method into the dataset upon which it should be used:

```
rmv.setInputFormat(dt);
```

Then, we will create a new dataset and apply `Filter.useFilter` method to it, providing the dataset to which the filter should be applied:

```
Instances nd = Filter.useFilter(dt, rmv);
```

Once we have done this, we'll create an object for the `ArffSaver` class; then, we'll assign the new dataset, nd, to the `ArffSaver` object, and name the object using the `setFile` method:

```
ArffSaver s = new ArffSaver();
s.setInstances(nd);
s.setFile(new File("fw.arff"));
```

Finally, we will write it to the disk by using the `writeBatch()` method:

```
s.writeBatch();
```

Run the code, and you will see the following output:

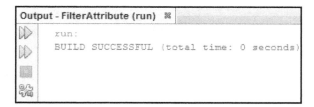

If the build is successful, we can compare both of the ARFF files, as shown in the following screenshot:

	weather.arff		fw.arff
1	@relation weather	1	@relation weather-weka.filters.unsupervised.attribute.Remove-R2
2		2	
3	@attribute outlook {sunny,overcast,rainy}	3	@attribute outlook {sunny,overcast,rainy}
4	@attribute temperature numeric	4	@attribute humidity numeric
5	@attribute humidity numeric	5	@attribute windy {TRUE,FALSE}
6	@attribute windy {TRUE,FALSE}	6	@attribute play {yes,no}
7	@attribute play {yes,no}	7	
8		8	@data
9	@data	9	sunny,85,FALSE,no
10	sunny,85,85,FALSE,no	10	sunny,90,TRUE,no
11	sunny,80,90,TRUE,no	11	overcast,86,FALSE,yes
12	overcast,83,86,FALSE,yes	12	rainy,96,FALSE,yes
13	rainy,70,96,FALSE,yes	13	rainy,80,FALSE,yes
14	rainy,68,80,FALSE,yes	14	rainy,70,TRUE,no
15	rainy,65,70,TRUE,no	15	overcast,65,TRUE,yes
16	overcast,64,65,TRUE,yes	16	sunny,95,FALSE,no
17	sunny,72,95,FALSE,no	17	sunny,70,FALSE,yes
18	sunny,69,70,FALSE,yes	18	rainy,80,FALSE,yes
19	rainy,75,80,FALSE,yes	19	sunny,70,TRUE,yes
20	sunny,75,70,TRUE,yes	20	overcast,90,TRUE,yes
21	overcast,72,90,TRUE,yes	21	overcast,75,FALSE,yes
22	overcast,81,75,FALSE,yes	22	rainy,91,TRUE,no
23	rainy,71,91,TRUE,no	23	

As you can see in the preceding screenshot, the `temperature` attribute has been removed from the new dataset (the `fw.arff` file). If we want to remove multiple attributes from the file, we use a dash (–) operator in the `String[] op = new String[]{"-R","2"};` part of the code.

For example, `String[] op = new String[]{"-R","2-3"};` will remove the attributes from 2 to 3. If we use 2–4 instead of 2–3, it will remove the attributes from 2 to 4 from the dataset.

Let's try to remove attributes using 2–4 and compare the files again, as follows:

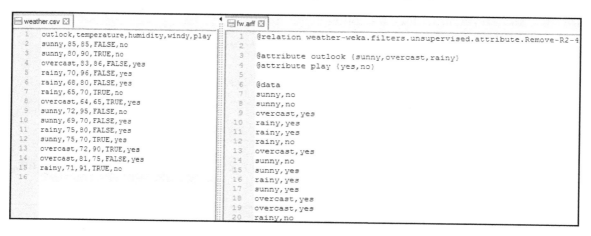

On the left-hand side, we can see the attributes that we have, and on the right-hand side, we can see the filtered attributes. This means that we have removed the second, third, and fourth attributes. We are left with the first and last attributes only.

That is how we can apply filtering to our dataset.

Discretizing attributes

We will now look at how to discretize attributes using Weka. First, let's explain what discretization is. **Discretizing attributes** means discretizing a range of numeric attributes in the dataset into nominal attributes. Hence, discretization is actually creating numeric data into categories. We will use binning for this; it skips the `class` attribute, if set.

Suppose that we have values from 1 to 60, and we want to categorize them into three different categories. Instead of creating numeric data, we want to create categorical data. We will create three bins. Let's create a bin for all of the values from 0 to 20, another bin for the values from 20 to 40, and a third bin for the values from 40 to 60. Every numeric data will become categorical data, using discretization.

We will now use the following options:

- `-B<num>`: This specifies the number of bins in which to divide the numeric attributes. The default value is 10.
- `-R(col1, col2-col4, ..)`: We have to assign the columns into which the binning should be done. `-R` helps us to create those bins. Please note that discretization will always work on numeric data, but it will not work on any nominal or other kind of data. `-R` specifies the list of columns to discretize. The first and last are valid indexes; if we do not specify anything, then the default is `first-last`.

Now, let's take a look at the code. We will use the classes that we have been using so far, which are `Instances`, `ArffSaver`, `File`, `DataSource`, and `Filter`, as follows:

```
import weka.core.Instances;
import weka.core.converters.ArffSaver;
import java.io.File;
import weka.core.converters.ConverterUtils.DataSource;
import weka.filters.Filter;
```

We will also use a new attribute, which is an unsupervised attribute from the `unsupervised.attribute` package. We will use the `Discretize` class from the `unsupervised.attribute` package:

```
import weka.filters.unsupervised.attribute.Discretize;
```

First, we'll read the dataset into our `src` object of our `DataSource` class; then, we will take it into the memory using the `dt` object of our `Instances` class. Once we have done this, we'll set the `options`. The first option that we'll set will be `-B`.

Let's suppose that we want to create 3 bins, and we want to apply discretization to the second and third attributes; the following code shows the options that need to be set:

```
DataSource src = new DataSource("weather.arff");
Instances dt = src.getDataSet();

String[] options = new String[4];
options[0] = "-B";
options[1] = "3";
options[2] = "-R";
options[3] = "2-3";
```

Then, we will create a dis object for the Discretize class, and we'll set these options to the Discretize class using setOptions method. We will then provide our dt object of our Instances class to the setInputFormat method, as follows:

```
Discretize dis = new Discretize();
dis.setOptions(options);
dis.setInputFormat(dt);
```

We will then create a new instance with the Filter.useFilter method, and we'll specify which dataset (dt) this filtering should be applied to, using what options; therefore, we'll include a dis object of Discretize class, as follows:

```
Instances nd = Filter.useFilter(dt, dis);
```

After that, we'll save it by using the ArffSaver class, and we'll provide the instances to ArffSaver using the setInstance method, and a new nd dataset. We'll provide the name to the ArffSaver class, which is weather-dis.arff, and we'll write it using the writeBatch method:

```
ArffSaver as = new ArffSaver();
as.setInstances(nd);
as.setFile(new File("weather-dis.arff"));
as.writeBatch();
```

Run the code. Once our build is successful, we'll see what actually happened. The following is our attribute in the weather.arff file:

```
weather.arff ☒

1    @relation weather
2
3    @attribute outlook {sunny,overcast,rainy}
4    @attribute temperature numeric
5    @attribute humidity numeric
6    @attribute windy {TRUE,FALSE}
7    @attribute play {yes,no}
8
9    @data
10   sunny,85,85,FALSE,no
11   sunny,80,90,TRUE,no
12   overcast,83,86,FALSE,yes
13   rainy,70,96,FALSE,yes
14   rainy,68,80,FALSE,yes
15   rainy,65,70,TRUE,no
16   overcast,64,65,TRUE,yes
17   sunny,72,95,FALSE,no
18   sunny,69,70,FALSE,yes
19   rainy,75,80,FALSE,yes
20   sunny,75,70,TRUE,yes
21   overcast,72,90,TRUE,yes
22   overcast,81,75,FALSE,yes
23   rainy,71,91,TRUE,no
```

We have applied binning to the second and third attributes, so the `temperature` and `humidity` attribute values will be converted into bins; we have asked for three bins to be created. Let's check whether it was done in the `weather-dis.arff` file, as shown in the following screenshot:

```
weather-dis.arff ☒

1    @relation weather-weka.filters.unsupervised.attribute.Discretize-B3-M-1.0-R2-3-precision6
2
3    @attribute outlook {sunny,overcast,rainy}
4    @attribute temperature {'\'(-inf-71]\'','\'(71-78]\'','\'(78-inf)\''}
5    @attribute humidity {'\'(-inf-75.333333]\'','\'(75.333333-85.666667]\'','\'(85.666667-inf)\''}
6    @attribute windy {TRUE,FALSE}
7    @attribute play {yes,no}
8
9    @data
10   sunny,'\'(78-inf)\'','\'(75.333333-85.666667]\'',FALSE,no
11   sunny,'\'(78-inf)\'','\'(85.666667-inf)\'',TRUE,no
12   overcast,'\'(78-inf)\'','\'(85.666667-inf)\'',FALSE,yes
13   rainy,'\'(-inf-71]\'','\'(85.666667-inf)\'',FALSE,yes
14   rainy,'\'(-inf-71]\'','\'(75.333333-85.666667]\'',FALSE,yes
15   rainy,'\'(-inf-71]\'','\'(-inf-75.333333]\'',TRUE,no
16   overcast,'\'(-inf-71]\'','\'(-inf-75.333333]\'',TRUE,yes
17   sunny,'\'(71-78]\'','\'(85.666667-inf)\'',FALSE,no
18   sunny,'\'(-inf-71]\'','\'(-inf-75.333333]\'',FALSE,yes
19   rainy,'\'(71-78]\'','\'(75.333333-85.666667]\'',FALSE,yes
20   sunny,'\'(71-78]\'','\'(-inf-75.333333]\'',TRUE,yes
21   overcast,'\'(71-78]\'','\'(85.666667-inf)\'',TRUE,yes
22   overcast,'\'(78-inf)\'','\'(-inf-75.333333]\'',FALSE,yes
23   rainy,'\'(-inf-71]\'','\'(85.666667-inf)\'',TRUE,no
```

We can see that we have created bins for the `temperature` and `humidity` attributes, which were numeric values. The bins that were created for `temperature` are `(inf-71]`,`( ' 71-78]`, and `(78-inf)`. For humidity, the bins are `(- inf-75.333333]`, `(75.333333-85.666667]`, and `(85.666667-inf)`. The values have also been converted into bins, as seen in the `@data` section.

If we want to create five bins instead of three bins, we can simply update the `options` code section as follows, and build the code:

```
options[0] = "-B";
options[1] = "5";
options[2] = "-R";
options[3] = "2-3";
```

Instead of three bins, we now have five bins for the `temperature` attribute and five bins for the `humidity` attribute, as seen in the following screenshot:

```
weather-dis.arff
1    @relation weather-weka.filters.unsupervised.attribute.Discretize-B5-M-1.0-R2-3-precision6
2
3    @attribute outlook {sunny,overcast,rainy}
4    @attribute temperature {'\'(-inf-68.2]\'','\'(68.2-72.4]\'','\'(72.4-76.6]\'','\'(76.6-80.8]\'','\'(80.8-inf)\''}
5    @attribute humidity {'\'(-inf-71.2]\'','\'(71.2-77.4]\'','\'(77.4-83.6]\'','\'(83.6-89.8]\'','\'(89.8-inf)\''}
6    @attribute windy {TRUE,FALSE}
7    @attribute play {yes,no}
8
9    @data
10   sunny,'\'(80.8-inf)\'','\'(83.6-89.8]\'',FALSE,no
11   sunny,'\'(76.6-80.8]\'','\'(89.8-inf)\'',TRUE,no
12   overcast,'\'(80.8-inf)\'','\'(83.6-89.8]\'',FALSE,yes
13   rainy,'\'(68.2-72.4]\'','\'(89.8-inf)\'',FALSE,yes
14   rainy,'\'(-inf-68.2]\'','\'(77.4-83.6]\'',FALSE,yes
15   rainy,'\'(-inf-68.2]\'','\'(-inf-71.2]\'',TRUE,no
16   overcast,'\'(-inf-68.2]\'','\'(-inf-71.2]\'',TRUE,yes
17   sunny,'\'(68.2-72.4]\'','\'(89.8-inf)\'',FALSE,no
18   sunny,'\'(68.2-72.4]\'','\'(-inf-71.2]\'',FALSE,yes
19   rainy,'\'(72.4-76.6]\'','\'(77.4-83.6]\'',FALSE,yes
20   sunny,'\'(72.4-76.6]\'','\'(-inf-71.2]\'',TRUE,yes
21   overcast,'\'(68.2-72.4]\'','\'(89.8-inf)\'',TRUE,yes
22   overcast,'\'(80.8-inf)\'','\'(71.2-77.4]\'',FALSE,yes
23   rainy,'\'(68.2-72.4]\'','\'(89.8-inf)\'',TRUE,no
```

This is how we can perform discretization and convert numeric data to categorical data.

Attribute selection

We will now look at how to perform attribute selection. **Attribute selection** is a technique for deciding which attributes are the most favorable attributes for performing classification or clustering.

So, let's take a look at the code and see what happens, as follows:

```
import weka.core.Instances;
import weka.core.converters.ArffSaver;
import java.io.File;
import weka.core.converters.ConverterUtils.DataSource;
import weka.filters.Filter;
import weka.filters.supervised.attribute.AttributeSelection;
import weka.attributeSelection.CfsSubsetEval;
import weka.attributeSelection.GreedyStepwise;
```

The first five classes will be the same as those we used earlier. We will also be using a new type of attribute, which will be a supervised attribute from the `filters.supervised` package, and the `AttributeSelection` class. Then, we have an `attribute.Selection` package, and from that, we'll be using the `CfsSubsetEval` class and the `GreedyStepwise` class.

In the following code, we'll first read the ARFF file into the `src` object of the `DataSource` class; then, we'll assign the `src` object to the `dt` object of the `Instance` class. We will then create objects for the `AttributeSelection`, `CfsSubsetEval`, and `GreedyStepwise` classes, as follows:

```
DataSource src = new
DataSource("/Users/admin/Documents/NetBeansProjects/Datasets/weather.arff")
;
Instances dt = src.getDataSet();
AttributeSelection asel = new AttributeSelection();
CfsSubsetEval evl = new CfsSubsetEval();
GreedyStepwise sh = new GreedyStepwise();
```

Then, we will assign the `evl` and `sh` objects of the `CfsSubsetEval` and `GreedyStepwise` (which is actually a search procedure) classes to the `asel` object of the `AttributeSelection` class. Then, we will assign the dataset, `dt`, to the `asel` object, as shown in the following code:

```
asel.setEvaluator(evl);
asel.setSearch(sh);
asel.setInputFormat(dt);
```

After that, we will create a new dataset; we'll use the `Filter.useFilter` method and give the name of the dataset (`dt`) to which the filtering should be done, and what options (`asel`) we want to perform the attribute selection with:

```
Instances nd = Filter.useFilter(dt, asel);
```

Finally, we'll create an `as` object for the `ArffSaver` class; we will assign the new dataset (`nd`) to the `as` object. We'll also assign the filename (`weather-sel.arff`) to the `as` object, and write it to the disk, as follows:

```
ArffSaver as = new ArffSaver();
as.setInstances(nd);
as.setFile(new File("weather-sel.arff"));
as.writeBatch();
```

Let's run the code and compare the `weather.arff` file and the newly generated dataset, as follows:

```
 weather.arff                                          weather-sel.arff
  1  @relation weather                          1  @relation 'weather-weka.filters.supervised.attribute.AttributeSelection-Eweka.attributeSelection.CfsSubsetEval -P
  2                                             2   1 -E 1-Sweka.attributeSelection.GreedyStepwise -T -1.7976931348623157E308 -N -1 -num-slots 1'
  3  @attribute outlook {sunny,overcast,rainy}  3
  4  @attribute temperature numeric             4  @attribute outlook {sunny,overcast,rainy}
  5  @attribute humidity numeric                5  @attribute windy {TRUE,FALSE}
  6  @attribute windy {TRUE,FALSE}              6  @attribute play {yes,no}
  7  @attribute play {yes,no}                   7
  8                                             8  @data
  9  @data                                      9  sunny,FALSE,no
 10  sunny,85,85,FALSE,no                       10  sunny,TRUE,no
 11  sunny,80,90,TRUE,no                        11  overcast,FALSE,yes
 12  overcast,83,86,FALSE,yes                   12  rainy,FALSE,yes
 13  rainy,70,96,FALSE,yes                      13  rainy,FALSE,yes
 14  rainy,68,80,FALSE,yes                      14  rainy,TRUE,no
 15  rainy,65,70,TRUE,no                        15  overcast,TRUE,yes
 16  overcast,64,65,TRUE,yes                    16  sunny,FALSE,no
 17  sunny,72,95,FALSE,no                       17  sunny,FALSE,yes
 18  sunny,69,70,FALSE,yes                      18  rainy,FALSE,yes
 19  rainy,75,80,FALSE,yes                      19  sunny,TRUE,yes
 20  sunny,75,70,TRUE,yes                       20  overcast,TRUE,yes
 21  overcast,72,90,TRUE,yes                    21  overcast,FALSE,yes
 22  overcast,81,75,FALSE,yes                   22  rainy,TRUE,no
 23  rainy,71,91,TRUE,no                        23
```

This file was created using attribute selection. The `GreedyStepwise` search decided that the two numeric attributes, `temperature` and `humidity`, are of the least significance to our classification/clustering algorithms, and removed them from the file.

Summary

In this chapter, you learned how to filter attributes, how to discretize attributes using binning, and how to apply attribute selection. The processes of filtering and discretizing attributes use unsupervised filters, whereas attribute selection is performed by using supervised filters.

In the next chapter, you'll see how to apply supervised learning.

6
Supervised Learning

In this chapter, we'll look at how to train, develop, evaluate, and make predictions with a classifier, and how to save, load, and make predictions with a model that we have developed.

We will cover the following topics in this chapter:

- Developing a classifier
- Model evaluation
- Making predictions
- Loading and saving models

Developing a classifier

We'll be developing a very simple, decision tree-based classifier, using the `weka.classifiers` package. For decision tree classification, we'll use the J48 algorithm, which is a very popular algorithm. To develop a classifier, we'll set two flags, as follows:

- `-C`: Sets the confidence threshold for pruning. Its default value is `0.25`.
- `-M`: Sets the maximum number of instances for developing a decision tree classifier. Its default value is `2`.

All of the other classifiers can be developed based on similar methods, which we'll incorporate while developing our decision tree classifier. We'll develop one more classifier—a Naive Bayes classifier—based on the same mechanism that we will follow to develop our decision tree classifier.

Let's get to the code and see how to do it. We'll start by importing the following classes:

```
import weka.core.Instances;
import weka.core.converters.ConverterUtils.DataSource;
import weka.classifiers.trees.J48;
```

Now, let's move on to the following code:

```
public static void main(String[] args) {
    // TODO code application logic here
    try{
        DataSource src = new
DataSource("/Users/admin/Documents/NetBeansProjects/DevelopClassifier/vote.
arff");
        Instances dt = src.getDataSet();
        dt.setClassIndex(dt.numAttributes()-1);
        String[] options = new String[4];
        options[0] = "-C";
        options[1] = "0.1";
        options[2] = "-M";
        options[3] = "2";
        J48 tree = new J48();
        tree.setOptions(options);
        tree.buildClassifier(dt);
        System.out.println(tree.getCapabilities().toString());
        System.out.println(tree.graph());
        //NaiveBayes nb = new NaiveBayes();
        }
    catch(Exception e){
        System.out.println("Error!!!!\n" + e.getMessage());
    }
}
```

This time, we're using a `vote.arff` dataset, because it has a very large amount of data. It is the 1984 United States Congressional Voting Records database, which has many tuples. It includes attributes such as whether a member is handicapped. Based on these attributes, it makes a prediction on whether a person is a Democrat or a Republican.

First, we'll create an object for our dataset by using a `DataSource` class. Then, we'll create an `Instances` object, and we'll put the dataset into the `Instances` object. Once we have opened our dataset, we will have to tell Weka which attribute is a class attribute (which one will be used for classification). As you can see in the list of attributes in the preceding code, the class attribute is at the end. Therefore, we'll take `setClassIndex`; and, since the −1 attribute is the class attribute, (`dt.numAttributed()-1`) will get the index of that particular attribute.

We'll then create an array of `Strings`; and, since we need to set −C and −M, we'll initialize our `String` array with four elements. The first element will be −C, the second will be the threshold value, the third will be −M, and the fourth will be the number of iterations it should take. Then, we will create an object for `J48`. Once we have created an object for `J48`, we'll assign the options to `J48` by using `setOptions`. Then, we will have to build a classifier using the dataset.

So, we will take our `J48` object with its `buildClassifier` method, and we'll supply it with our dataset. This will create a classifier for the `tree` object.

Once we have done this, we can print its capabilities with the `toString` method. This will print the types of attributes that it can classify. Once we have done so, we can print its graph. This will give us the exact decision tree graph that it has developed, which it has also trained.

Running the code will provide the following output:

```
run:
Capabilities: [Nominal attributes, Binary attributes, Unary attributes, Empty nominal attributes, Numeric attributes, Date attributes, Missing values, Nominal class]
Dependencies: []
interfaces: [Drawable, PartitionGenerator, Sourcable, WeightedInstancesHandler]
Minimum number of instances: 0

digraph J48Tree {
N0 [label="physician-fee-freeze" ]
N0->N1 [label="= n"]
N1 [label="democrat (253.41/3.75)" shape=box style=filled ]
N0->N2 [label="= y"]
N2 [label="synfuels-corporation-cutback" ]
N2->N3 [label="= n"]
N3 [label="republican (145.71/4.0)" shape=box style=filled ]
N2->N4 [label="= y"]
N4 [label="mx-missile" ]
N4->N5 [label="= n"]
N5 [label="adoption-of-the-budget-resolution" ]
N5->N6 [label="= n"]
N6 [label="republican (22.61/3.32)" shape=box style=filled ]
N5->N7 [label="= y"]
N7 [label="anti-satellite-test-ban" ]
N7->N8 [label="= n"]
N8 [label="democrat (5.04/0.02)" shape=box style=filled ]
N7->N9 [label="= y"]
N9 [label="republican (2.21)" shape=box style=filled ]
N4->N10 [label="= y"]
N10 [label="democrat (6.03/1.03)" shape=box style=filled ]
}

BUILD SUCCESSFUL (total time: 0 seconds)
```

Since the first print statement was `getCapabilities`, that has been printed. The classifier has been trained, and it can incorporate `Nominal`, `Binary`, `Unary`, and a list of some more attributes that it can train itself on. `digraph J48Tree` in the output is the tree that was generated with those attributes. That is how we can develop a classifier.

Suppose that we want to train one more classifier, using Naive Bayes; first, we will have to incorporate the `NaiveBayes` class that is available in the `bayes` package of the `weka.classifiers` class:

```
import weka.classifiers.bayes.NaiveBayes;
```

Next, we will create an object, nb, for `NaiveBayes`, and pass the dt dataset to the `buildClassifier` method of nb:

```
NaiveBayes nb = new NaiveBayes();
nb.buildClassifier(dt);
System.out.println(nb.getCapabilities().toString());
```

When this has finished, the classifier will be trained, and we will be able to print its capabilities.

Run the code again to get the following output:

```
run:
Capabilities: [Nominal attributes, Binary attributes, Unary attributes, Empty nominal attributes, Numeric attributes, Date attributes, Missing values, Nominal class, Binary class, Mis
Dependencies: []
Interfaces: [Drawable, PartitionGenerator, Sourcable, WeightedInstancesHandler]
Minimum number of instances: 0

digraph J48Tree {
N0 [label="physician-fee-freeze" ]
N0->N1 [label="= n"]
N1 [label="democrat (253.41/3.75)" shape=box style=filled ]
N0->N2 [label="= y"]
N2 [label="synfuels-corporation-cutback" ]
N2->N3 [label="= n"]
N3 [label="republican (145.71/4.0)" shape=box style=filled ]
N2->N4 [label="= y"]
N4 [label="mx-missile" ]
N4->N5 [label="= n"]
N5 [label="adoption-of-the-budget-resolution" ]
N5->N6 [label="= n"]
N6 [label="republican (22.61/3.32)" shape=box style=filled ]
N5->N7 [label="= y"]
N7 [label="anti-satellite-test-ban" ]
N7->N8 [label="= n"]
N8 [label="democrat (5.04/0.02)" shape=box style=filled ]
N7->N9 [label="= y"]
N9 [label="republican (2.21)" shape=box style=filled ]
N4->N10 [label="= y"]
N10 [label="democrat (6.03/1.03)" shape=box style=filled ]
}

Capabilities: [Nominal attributes, Binary attributes, Unary attributes, Empty nominal attributes, Numeric attributes, Missing values, Nominal class, Binary class, Missing class values
Dependencies: []
Interfaces: [WeightedAttributesHandler, WeightedInstancesHandler]
Minimum number of instances: 0

BUILD SUCCESSFUL (total time: 0 seconds)
```

In the preceding screenshot, you can see that the Naive Bayes classifier has been trained, and it has provided the attributes upon which the classifier can be trained.

Model evaluation

We will now look at how to evaluate the classifier that we have trained. Let's start with the code.

We'll start by importing the following classes:

```
import weka.core.Instances;
import weka.core.converters.ConverterUtils.DataSource;
import weka.classifiers.trees.J48;
import weka.classifiers.Evaluation;
import java.util.Random;
```

This time, we'll use the Evaluation class from the weka.classifiers package, and a Random class for some random value generation.

The DataSource that we'll be using is the segment-challenge.arff file. We are using this because it has a test dataset, and it is also one of the datasets that comes with Weka. We'll assign it to our Instances object, and we will then tell Weka which attribute is the class attribute. We'll set the flags for our decision tree classifier and create an object for our decision tree classifier. Then, we'll set the options, and we'll build the classifier. We performed the same in the previous section:

```
public static void main(String[] args) {
    try {
        DataSource src = new
DataSource("/Users/admin/Documents/NetBeansProjects/ModelEvaluation/segment
-challenge.arff");
        Instances dt = src.getDataSet();
        dt.setClassIndex(dt.numAttributes()- 1);

        String[] options = new String[4];
        options[0] = "-C";
        options[1] = "0.1";
        options[2] = "-M";
        options[3] = "2";
        J48 mytree = new J48();
        mytree.setOptions(options);
        mytree.buildClassifier(dt);
```

Next, we'll create an object for the Evaluation and Random classes. Once we have done this, we'll create a new DataSource object, src1, for our test dataset, and a segment-test.arff file. We'll assign this to a new Instances object, and we'll tell Weka which particular attribute is a class attribute. Then, we'll use the eval.evaluateModel object and a classifier that we have trained with the new test dataset that we want to evaluate:

```
        Evaluation eval = new Evaluation(dt);
        Random rand = new Random(1);

        DataSource src1 = new
DataSource("/Users/admin/Documents/NetBeansProjects/ModelEvaluation/segment
-test.arff");
        Instances tdt = src1.getDataSet();
        tdt.setClassIndex(tdt.numAttributes() - 1);
        eval.evaluateModel(mytree, tdt);
```

When this has finished, we can print the Evaluation results, as follows:

```
        System.out.println(eval.toSummaryString("Evaluation
results:\n", false));
```

As you can see in the preceding code, we get the `Evaluation` results by using the `toSummaryString` method. If we want to print them individually, we can type the following code:

```
System.out.println("Correct % = " + eval.pctCorrect());
System.out.println("Incorrect % = " + eval.pctIncorrect());
System.out.println("kappa = " + eval.kappa());
System.out.println("MAE = " + eval.meanAbsoluteError());
System.out.println("RMSE = " + eval.rootMeanSquaredError());
System.out.println("RAE = " + eval.relativeAbsoluteError());
System.out.println("Precision = " + eval.precision(1));
System.out.println("Recall = " + eval.recall(1));
System.out.println("fMeasure = " + eval.fMeasure(1));
System.out.println(eval.toMatrixString("=== Overall Confusion
Matrix ==="));
```

At the end, we'll print the confusion matrix. Run the code to get the following output:

```
Output - ModelEvaluation (run)

run:
Evaluation results:

Correctly Classified Instances         781              96.4198 %
Incorrectly Classified Instances        29               3.5802 %
Kappa statistic                          0.9582
Mean absolute error                      0.0138
Root mean squared error                  0.0968
Relative absolute error                  5.6391 %
Root relative squared error             27.6379 %
Total Number of Instances              810

Correct % = 96.41975308641975
Incorrect % = 3.580246913580247
kappa = 0.9581767260335192
MAE = 0.013820948362838705
RMSE = 0.09680895742215871
RAE = 5.639126704284399
Precision = 1.0
Recall = 1.0
fMeasure = 1.0
=== Overall Confusion Matrix ===
    a   b   c   d   e   f   g   <-- classified as
  124   0   0   0   1   0   0 |   a = brickface
    0 110   0   0   0   0   0 |   b = sky
    3   0 116   1   2   0   0 |   c = foliage
    1   0   0 107   2   0   0 |   d = cement
    2   0  10   3 110   0   1 |   e = window
    0   0   0   0   0  94   0 |   f = path
    0   0   1   0   0   2 120 |   g = grass

BUILD SUCCESSFUL (total time: 0 seconds)
```

The `toSummaryString` method has printed all of the values. The values have been printed individually, using `pctCorrect`, `pctIncorrect`, `kappa`, `meanAbsoluteError`, and so on. Finally, we have printed the confusion matrix.

124 instances have been correctly classified for a, and the machine has classified 6 more for a, which were either c, d, or e. Similarly, for b, 110 instances were correctly classified, and there were only 110 instances of b. There were 125 instances of a; out of those, the machine classified 124, and so on. This is how we create a confusion matrix and perform evaluation on our classifier.

Making predictions

Now, we'll look at how to predict a class using our test dataset. Let's start with the code. We'll use the following packages:

```
import weka.core.Instances;
import weka.core.converters.ConverterUtils.DataSource;
import weka.classifiers.trees.J48;
import weka.core.Instance;
```

Notice that this time, we'll be using a new class: an `Instance` class from the `weka.core` package. This will help us to predict the class, using our test dataset. Then, as usual, we'll be reading our dataset into the `src` object, and we'll assign it to a `dt` object. We'll tell Weka which class attribute will be setting the attributes for our decision tree classifier in this dataset. Then, we'll create a decision tree classifier, set the objects for our decision tree classifier, and build the classifier, as follows:

```
public static void main(String[] args) {
    // TODO code application logic here
    try {
        DataSource src = new
DataSource("/Users/admin/Documents/NetBeansProjects/MakingPredictions/segme
nt-challenge.arff");
        Instances dt = src.getDataSet();
        dt.setClassIndex(dt.numAttributes() - 1);

        String[] options = new String[4];
        options[0] = "-C";
        options[1] = "0.1";
        options[2] = "-M";
        options[3] = "2";
        J48 mytree = new J48();
        mytree.setOptions(options);
        mytree.buildClassifier(dt);
```

Next, we'll create a new `src1` object for the `DataSource` class, where we will provide our `segment-test` dataset. We'll assign it to a new `tdt` object, which will take it into the memory. Then, we will have to set the target variable again, using the `setClassIndex` method. Once we have done this, we will be good to go:

```
DataSource src1 = new
DataSource("/Users/admin/Documents/NetBeansProjects/MakingPredictions/segme
nt-test.arff");
Instances tdt = src1.getDataSet();
tdt.setClassIndex(tdt.numAttributes()-1);

System.out.println("ActualClass \t ActualValue \t PredictedValue \t
PredictedClass");
for (int i = 0; i < tdt.numInstances(); i++)
{
    String act =
tdt.instance(i).stringValue(tdt.instance(i).numAttributes()-1);
    double actual = tdt.instance(i).classValue();
    Instance inst = tdt.instance(i);
    double predict = mytree.classifyInstance(inst);
    String pred = inst.toString(inst .numAttributes()-1);
    System.out.println(act + " \t\t " + actual + " \t\t " + predict + "
\t\t " + pred);
}
```

Now, we want to get the actual class and the predicted class. Weka only assigns a value to the actual and predicted classes; hence, we'll print the following four things:

- The actual class
- The actual value
- The predicted value
- The predicted class

Since we have *n* number of rows in our test dataset, we'll execute the rows one by one. Therefore, we'll use a `for` loop, from `0` to the number of instances that we have in our test dataset. We'll first assign the actual class to a `String` object. Using that, we'll take our `tdt.instance` and set a value. Then, we'll take the ith attribute, and we'll print the class attribute. After that, we'll create an `actual` variable, which will be of the `double` type, and we will print its class value using the `classValue` method. Once we have done this, we will create an object for that particular dataset's i^{th} instance. Then, we'll create a `predict` variable. It should be of the `double` type. We'll classify it by using our tree object with a `classifyInstance` method. We'll assign the `inst` object to it; this will have our `predict` class value. Now, since we have a class value, we can convert it into a string by using the `toString` method, and, finally, we can print all four values.

Running the code will provide the following output:

```
Output - MakingPredictions (run)
  run:
  ActualClass      ActualValue      PredictedValue           PredictedClass
  cement           3.0              3.0              cement
  path             5.0              5.0              path
  grass            6.0              6.0              grass
  grass            6.0              6.0              grass
  window           4.0              4.0              window
  foliage                   2.0                   2.0               foliage
  brickface                 0.0                   0.0               brickface
  path             5.0              5.0              path
  grass            6.0              6.0              grass
  grass            6.0              6.0              grass
  cement           3.0              3.0              cement
  grass            6.0              6.0              grass
  path             5.0              5.0              path
  window           4.0              4.0              window
  foliage                   2.0                   2.0               foliage
  brickface                 0.0                   0.0               brickface
  brickface                 0.0                   0.0               brickface
  window           4.0              4.0              window
  brickface                 0.0                   0.0               brickface
  sky              1.0              1.0              sky
  cement           3.0              3.0              cement
  sky              1.0              1.0              sky
  grass            6.0              6.0              grass
  grass            6.0              6.0              grass
  brickface                 0.0                   0.0               brickface
  window           4.0              4.0              window
  window           4.0              2.0              window
  window           4.0              4.0              window
  sky              1.0              1.0              sky
  path             5.0              5.0              path
  grass            6.0              6.0              grass
  sky              1.0              1.0              sky
  sky              1.0              1.0              sky
```

As we expected, we can see the `ActualClass`, `ActualValue`, `PredictedClass`, and `PredictedValue`. That is how predictions are performed.

Loading and saving models

Now, we will look at how to save a model that we have trained, and then load that model onto a hard disk. So, let's quickly get to the code.

In this particular section, we'll be saving a model; so, we'll use the following three classes:

```
import weka.core.Instances;
import weka.core.converters.ConverterUtils.DataSource;
import weka.classifiers.trees.J48;
```

We'll take the ARFF file into our `src` object (of the `DataSource` class), and we'll assign it to the `dt` object of the `Instances` class. Then, we'll assign the `src` object to our `dt` object; in the `dt` object, we'll indicate which particular attribute is a class attribute. We'll set certain `options` for our decision tree classifier, and we'll create an object for our decision tree classifier. Then, we'll set options for it, and we'll build it:

```
public static void main(String[] args) {
    // TODO code application logic here
    try {
        DataSource src = new
DataSource("/Users/admin/Documents/NetBeansProjects/SaveModel/segment-
challenge.arff");
        Instances dt = src.getDataSet();
        dt.setClassIndex(dt.numAttributes() - 1);

        String[] options = new String[4];
        options[0] = "-C";
        options[1] = "0.1";
        options[2] = "-M";
        options[3] = "2";
        J48 mytree = new J48();
        mytree.setOptions(options);
        mytree.buildClassifier(dt);
```

Once we have built our decision tree classifier, we will save it to our hard disk. To do so, we'll use the following method:

```
weka.core.SerializationHelper.write("/Users/admin/Documents/NetBeansProject
s/SaveModel/myDT.model", mytree);
```

We'll name the model `myDT.model`, and we'll provide an object to it: `mytree`. Therefore, the classifier that we have trained will be saved to our hard disk with the name `myDT.model`.

Run the code to get the following output:

If the build is successful, the classifier will be saved to the hard disk. If we want to confirm it, we can check it on the hard disk.

Now, we want to load the classifier from the hard disk. The name of the classifier is myDT.model. We will use the first four classes, as follows:

```
import weka.core.Instances;
import weka.core.converters.ConverterUtils.DataSource;
import weka.classifiers.trees.J48;
import weka.core.Instance;
```

This time, we want to read them to make certain predictions. We'll create an object for our decision tree, and we'll typecast it. Since Weka does not know which classifier (of which model) is being loaded, first, we have to typecast it using a particular class, as shown in the following code:

```
public static void main(String[] args) {
    // TODO code application logic here
    try{
        J48 mytree = (J48)
weka.core.SerializationHelper.read("/Users/admin/Documents/NetBeansProjects
/LoadModel/myDT.model");
        DataSource src1 = new
DataSource("/Users/admin/Documents/NetBeansProjects/LoadModel/segment-
test.arff");
        Instances tdt = src1.getDataSet();
        tdt.setClassIndex(tdt.numAttributes() - 1);
        System.out.println("ActualClass \t ActualValue \t PredictedValue \t
PredictedClass");
        for (int i = 0; i < tdt.numInstances(); i++) {
            String act =
tdt.instance(i).stringValue(tdt.instance(i).numAttributes() - 1);
            double actual = tdt.instance(i).classValue();
            Instance inst = tdt.instance(i);
            double predict = mytree.classifyInstance(inst);
            String pred = inst.toString(inst.numAttributes() - 1);
            System.out.println(act + " \t\t " + actual + " \t\t " + predict
+ " \t\t " + pred);
        }
    }
    catch(Exception e){
        System.out.println("Error!!!!\n" + e.getMessage());
    }
}
```

Then, we will take `weka.core.SerializationHelper`; this time, we'll use a `read` method and name the classifier or the complete path with the name of the classifier. Then, we'll create a `DataSource` object and we'll assign our test dataset to our `Instances`, and we'll tell Weka which particular attribute is the target attribute. Then, we'll take the four values that we want to print (from the last chapter). We will take a `for` loop for all of the instances of the test dataset, print the `ActualClass`, print the `ActualValue`, and initialize the object for `Instance`. We'll take the `Instance` object, and we'll provide it with the test dataset's i[th] instance; we'll make the predictions by using the `classifyInstance` method. Once we have done this, we'll print its `String`, we'll assign the `String` to `pred`, and we'll print all of the values.

Running the code will provide the following output:

```
Output - LoadModel (run)

run:
ActualClass       ActualValue       PredictedValue       PredictedClass
cement            3.0               3.0                  cement
path              5.0               5.0                  path
grass             6.0               6.0                  grass
grass             6.0               6.0                  grass
window            4.0               4.0                  window
foliage                     2.0               2.0                  foliage
brickface                   0.0               0.0                  brickface
path              5.0               5.0                  path
grass             6.0               6.0                  grass
grass             6.0               6.0                  grass
cement            3.0               3.0                  cement
grass             6.0               6.0                  grass
path              5.0               5.0                  path
window            4.0               4.0                  window
foliage                     2.0               2.0                  foliage
brickface                   0.0               0.0                  brickface
brickface                   0.0               0.0                  brickface
window            4.0               4.0                  window
brickface                   0.0               0.0                  brickface
sky               1.0               1.0                  sky
cement            3.0               3.0                  cement
sky               1.0               1.0                  sky
grass             6.0               6.0                  grass
grass             6.0               6.0                  grass
brickface                   0.0               0.0                  brickface
window            4.0               4.0                  window
window            4.0               2.0                  window
window            4.0               4.0                  window
sky               1.0               1.0                  sky
path              5.0               5.0                  path
grass             6.0               6.0                  grass
sky               1.0               1.0                  sky
sky               1.0               1.0                  sky
```

Summary

In this chapter, you learned how to develop and evaluate a classifier. You also learned how to make predictions using a trained model, and how to save that particular model to a hard disk. Then, you learned how to load the model from a hard disk, in order to use it for future purposes.

In the next chapter, we will look at how to perform semi-supervised and unsupervised learning.

7
Semi-Supervised and Unsupervised Learning

In this chapter, we'll look at how to build and evaluate an unsupervised model. We'll also look at semi-supervised learning, the difference between unsupervised and semi-supervised learning, how to build a semi-supervised model, and how to make predictions using a semi-supervised model.

In this chapter, we'll cover the following topics:

- Working with k-means clustering
- Evaluating a clustering model
- Distance matrix formation using cosine similarity
- The difference between unsupervised and semi-supervised learning
- Self-training and co-training machine learning models
- Making predictions with semi-supervised machine learning models

Working with k-means clustering

Let's look at how to build a clustering model. We'll be building an unsupervised model using k-means clustering.

We will use the `Instances` class and the `DataSource` class, just as we did in previous chapters. Since we are working with clustering, we will use the `weka.clusterers` package to import the `SimpleKMeans` class, as follows:

```
import weka.core.Instances;
import weka.core.converters.ConverterUtils.DataSource;
import weka.clusterers.SimpleKMeans;
```

First, we'll read our ARFF file into a dataset object, and we'll assign it to an `Instances` object. Now, since this is all we have to do (in classification we had to also assign the target variable, the class attribute), we have to tell Weka what the class attribute is, then we will create an object for our k-means clustering. First, we have to tell Weka how many clusters we want to create. Let's suppose that we want to create three clusters. We'll take our k-means object and set `setNumClusters` to `3`; then, we'll build our cluster using `buildClusterer`, and we'll assign the dataset into which the cluster will be done. Then, we'll print our model, as follows:

```
public static void main(String[] args) {
    // TODO code application logic here
    try{
        DataSource src = new
DataSource("/Users/admin/Documents/NetBeansProjects/Datasets/weather.arff")
;
        Instances dt = src.getDataSet();
        SimpleKMeans model = new SimpleKMeans();
        model.setNumClusters(3);
        model.buildClusterer(dt);
        System.out.println(model);
    }
    catch(Exception e){
        System.out.println(e.getMessage());
    }
}
```

After running it, we will see the following output:

```
Output - Clustering (run)

run:

kMeans
======

Number of iterations: 2
Within cluster sum of squared errors: 20.0

Initial starting points (random):

Cluster 0: rainy,mild,normal,FALSE,yes
Cluster 1: overcast,cool,normal,TRUE,yes
Cluster 2: rainy,mild,high,TRUE,no

Missing values globally replaced with mean/mode

Final cluster centroids:
                                 Cluster#
Attribute        Full Data          0          1          2
                   (14.0)        (7.0)      (3.0)      (4.0)
=============================================================
outlook             sunny        rainy   overcast      sunny
temperature          mild         mild       cool        hot
humidity             high       normal     normal       high
windy               FALSE        FALSE       TRUE       TRUE
play                  yes          yes        yes         no



BUILD SUCCESSFUL (total time: 0 seconds)
```

In the preceding screenshot, we can see that, initially, three clusters were created with initial values. After performing the clustering, we get the final three clusters, so that Cluster 0 has 7.0 values, Cluster 1 has 3.0 values, and Cluster 2 has 4.0 values. Since we are not providing a class for our clustering algorithm, the string actually tries to divide similar-looking data into groups (which we call clusters). This is how clustering is done.

Evaluating a clustering model

Now, we'll look at how to evaluate a clustering model that has been trained. Let's look at the code and see how this is done.

We'll be using the following classes:

```
import weka.core.Instances;
import weka.core.converters.ConverterUtils.DataSource;
import weka.clusterers.SimpleKMeans;
import weka.clusterers.ClusterEvaluation;
```

We'll use the `ClusterEvaluation` class from the `weka.clusterers` package for evaluation.

First, we will read our dataset into our `DataSource` object and assign it to the `Instances` object. Then, we'll create our k-means object and specify the number of clusters that we want to create. Next, we will train our clustering algorithm using the `buildClusterer` method; then, we'll print it using `println`. This is similar to what you saw earlier:

```
public static void main(String[] args) {
    // TODO code application logic here
    try{
        DataSource src = new
DataSource("/Users/admin/Documents/NetBeansProjects/ClusterEval/weather.arf
f");
        Instances dt = src.getDataSet();
        SimpleKMeans model = new SimpleKMeans();
        model.setNumClusters(3);
        model.buildClusterer(dt);
        System.out.println(model);
```

Next, we'll create an object for the `ClusterEvaluation` class. Then, we'll read in a new test dataset and assign it to our `DataSource` object. Finally, we'll take it into the memory by using our `Instances` object, and we will set the `Clusterer` model using `setClusterer` and pass the trained `Clusterer` object to the `setClusterer` method. Once we have done this, we will need to evaluate the cluster; so, we will have to pass the test dataset to the `evaluateClusterer` method. Then, we will print the resulting strings, so that we can get the number of clusters that we have trained:

```
        ClusterEvaluation eval = new ClusterEvaluation();
        DataSource src1 = new
DataSource("/Users/admin/Documents/NetBeansProjects/ClusterEval/weather.tes
t.arff");
```

```
Instances tdt = src1.getDataSet();
eval.setClusterer(model);
eval.evaluateClusterer(tdt);
```

Running the preceding code will result in the following output:

```
run:

kMeans                                            kMeans
======                                            ======


Number of iterations: 2                           Number of iterations: 2
Within cluster sum of squared errors: 20.0        Within cluster sum of squared errors: 20.0


Initial starting points (random):                 Initial starting points (random):

Cluster 0: rainy,mild,normal,FALSE,yes            Cluster 0: rainy,mild,normal,FALSE,yes
Cluster 1: overcast,cool,normal,TRUE,yes          Cluster 1: overcast,cool,normal,TRUE,yes
Cluster 2: rainy,mild,high,TRUE,no                Cluster 2: rainy,mild,high,TRUE,no


Missing values globally replaced with mean/mode   Missing values globally replaced with mean/mode


Final cluster centroids:                          Final cluster centroids:
                         Cluster#                                           Cluster#
Attribute   Full Data       0       1        2    Attribute   Full Data       0       1        2
            (14.0)      (7.0)   (3.0)    (4.0)                 (14.0)      (7.0)   (3.0)    (4.0)
===========================================       ==============================================
outlook      sunny       rainy  overcast   sunny  outlook      sunny       rainy  overcast   sunny
temperature  mild        mild     cool       hot  temperature  mild        mild     cool       hot
humidity     high        normal normal      high  humidity     high        normal normal      high
windy        FALSE       FALSE    TRUE      TRUE   windy        FALSE       FALSE    TRUE      TRUE
play         yes         yes      yes         no  play         yes         yes      yes         no


                                                  Clustered Instances

                                                  0      2 ( 22%)
                                                  1      3 ( 33%)
                                                  2      4 ( 44%)

                                                  # of clusters: 3
                                                  BUILD SUCCESSFUL (total time: 0 seconds)
```

We now have the number of clusters, which were printed individually, using our `eval` object. So, the values for the clusters are as follows: `22%` for the first cluster, `33%` for the second cluster, and `44%` for the third cluster. The total number of clusters is `3`.

An introduction to semi-supervised learning

Semi-supervised learning is a class of supervised learning that takes unlabeled data into consideration. If we have a very large amount of data, we most likely want to apply learning to it. However, training that particular data with supervised learning is a problem, because a supervised learning algorithm always requires a target variable: a class that can be assigned to the dataset.

Suppose that we have millions of instances of a particular type of data. Assigning a class to these instances would be a very big problem. Therefore, we'll take a small set from that particular data and manually tag the data (meaning that we'll manually provide a class for the data). Once we have done this, we'll train our model with it, so that we can work with the unlabeled data (because we now have a small set of labeled data, which we created). Typically, a small amount of labeled data is used with a large amount of unlabeled data. Semi-supervised learning falls between supervised and unsupervised learning, because we are taking a small amount of data that has been labeled and training our model with it; we are then trying to assign classes by using the trained model on the unlabeled data.

Many machine learning researchers have found that unlabeled data, when used in conjunction with a small amount of labeled data, can produce considerable improvements in learning accuracy. This is how semi-supervised learning works: with a combination of supervised learning and unsupervised learning, wherein we take a very small amount of data, label it, try to classify it, and then try to fit the unlabeled data into the labeled data.

The difference between unsupervised and semi-supervised learning

In this section, we'll look at the differences between unsupervised learning and semi-supervised learning.

Unsupervised learning develops a model based on unlabeled data, whereas semi-supervised learning employs both labeled and unlabeled data.

We use expected maximization, hierarchical clustering, and k-means clustering algorithms in unsupervised learning, whereas in semi-supervised learning, we apply either active learning or bootstrapping algorithms.

In Weka, we can perform semi-supervised learning using the `collective-classification` package. We will look at installing the `collective-classification` package later in this chapter, and you'll see how you can perform semi-supervised learning using collective classification.

Self-training and co-training machine learning models

You will now learn how to develop semi-supervised models.

The very first thing that we'll do is download a package for semi-supervised learning, then we will create a classifier for a semi-supervised model.

Downloading a semi-supervised package

Go to `https://github.com/fracpete/collective-classification-weka-package` to get the `collective-classification` Weka package. This is a semi-supervised learning package that is available in Weka.

There are two ways to install the package, as follows:

- Download the source from GitHub and compile it, then create a JAR file
- Go to the Weka package manager, and install the collective classification from there

After performing one of the preceding methods, you'll have a JAR file. You will need this JAR file to train the classifier. The source code that we'll be getting will provide the JAR file with the code. Let's look at how this is done.

Creating a classifier for semi-supervised models

Let's start with the following code:

```
import weka.core.Instances;
import weka.core.converters.ConverterUtils.DataSource;
import weka.classifiers.collective.functions.LLGC;
```

The very first things that we need are the `Instances` and `DataSource` classes, which we have been using since the beginning. The third class that we need is an `LLGC` class, which is available in the `functions` package of the `collective-classification` JAR file.

Therefore, we need to import two JAR files into the project; one is the conventional `weka.jar` file that we have already been using, and the second one is the semi-supervised learning file, the `collective-classification-<date>.jar` file, as seen in the following screenshot:

Now, we will create a `DataSource` object, and we'll assign our ARFF file to the `DataSource` object, as follows:

```
try{
    DataSource src = new DataSource("weather.arff");
    Instances dt = src.getDataSet();
    dt.setClassIndex(dt.numAttributes()-1);

    LLGC model = new LLGC();
    model.buildClassifier(dt);
    System.out.println(model.getCapabilities());
    }
catch(Exception e){
    System.out.println("Error!!!!\n" + e.getMessage());
    }
```

Then, we will create an `Instances` object, and we will assign the ARFF file to this `Instances` object and get our data into the memory. Once our dataset is available in the memory, we'll tell Weka which attribute is the class attribute that we have been using in the classification. Next, we will initialize the `LLGC` object. `LLGC` is a class for performing semi-supervised learning. We will use `model.buildClassifier(dt)`, and we will print the capabilities of the classifier.

The capabilities will be printed, as shown in the following screenshot:

```
Output - SemiSuperClassifier (run)
  run:
  Capabilities: [Nominal attributes, Binary attributes, Unary attributes, Empty nominal attributes, Numeric attributes, Date attributes, Missing values,
  Dependencies: []
  Interfaces: [Randomizable]
  Minimum number of instances: 1

  BUILD SUCCESSFUL (total time: 0 seconds)
```

As you can see in the preceding screenshot, these are the attributes that the LLGC class can perform the semi-supervised learning on, in order to build a model. This is how we will build a semi-supervised model.

Making predictions with semi-supervised machine learning models

Now, we'll look into how to make predictions using our trained model. Consider the following code:

```
import weka.core.Instances;
import weka.core.converters.ConverterUtils.DataSource;
import weka.classifiers.collective.functions.LLGC;
import weka.classifiers.collective.evaluation.Evaluation;
```

We will be importing two JAR libraries, as follows:

- The weka.jar library
- The collective-classification-<date>.jar library

Therefore, we will take the two base classes, Instances and DataSource, and we will use the LLGC class (since we have trained our model using LLGC) from the collective-classifications package, as well as the Evaluation class from the collective-classifications package.

We will first assign an ARFF file to our DataSource object; we'll read it into the memory, in an Instances object. We'll assign a class attribute to our Instances object, and then, we will build our model:

```
public static void main(String[] args) {
    try{
        DataSource src = new DataSource("weather.arff");
        Instances dt = src.getDataSet();
        dt.setClassIndex(dt.numAttributes()-1);
```

```
            LLGC model = new LLGC();
            model.buildClassifier(dt);
            System.out.println(model.getCapabilities());

            Evaluation eval = new Evaluation(dt);
            DataSource src1 = new DataSource("weather.test.arff");
            Instances tdt = src1.getDataSet();
            tdt.setClassIndex(tdt.numAttributes()-1);
            eval.evaluateModel(model, tdt);

            System.out.println(eval.toSummaryString("Evaluation results:\n",
    false));

            System.out.println("Correct % = "+eval.pctCorrect());
            System.out.println("Incorrect % = "+eval.pctIncorrect());
            System.out.println("AUC = "+eval.areaUnderROC(1));
            System.out.println("kappa = "+eval.kappa());
            System.out.println("MAE = "+eval.meanAbsoluteError());
            System.out.println("RMSE = "+eval.rootMeanSquaredError());
            System.out.println("RAE = "+eval.relativeAbsoluteError());
            System.out.println("RRSE = "+eval.rootRelativeSquaredError());
            System.out.println("Precision = "+eval.precision(1));
            System.out.println("Recall = "+eval.recall(1));
            System.out.println("fMeasure = "+eval.fMeasure(1));
            System.out.println("Error Rate = "+eval.errorRate());
            //the confusion matrix
            System.out.println(eval.toMatrixString("=== Overall Confusion
    Matrix ===\n"));
        }
        catch(Exception e)
        {
            System.out.println("Error!!!!\n" + e.getMessage());
        }
    }
}
```

Once we have done this, we will create an object for our `Evaluation` class, and we'll specify which dataset we want to perform the evaluation on. Hence, we'll pass our dataset to the `Evaluation` class constructor. Then, we will create a new object for `DataSource` class, and we will take the `weather.test.arff` file for testing. We will create an `Instances` object, `tdt`, and assign the dataset to the test dataset, `tdt`.

Then, we will need to inform Weka which attribute in the `tdt` object is our class attribute; therefore, we will call the `setClassIndex` method. Then, we will use the `evaluateModel` method of our `Evaluation` class and pass in the `model` and our test dataset.

Once this is done, we will print the `Evaluation` results all at once; or, if you want, you can individually print the results, as we did in the semi-supervised learning exercise.

Let's run the code. We will get the following output:

```
Output - SuperSupervised (run)

run:
Capabilities: [Nominal attributes, Binary attributes, Unary attributes, Empty nominal attributes, Numeric attributes, Date attributes,
Dependencies: []
Interfaces: [Randomizable]
Minimum number of instances: 1

WARNING: No splitting will be performed, test = train!
Evaluation results:

Correctly Classified Instances          4                 44.4444 %
Incorrectly Classified Instances        5                 55.5556 %
Kappa statistic                         0
Mean absolute error                     0.5556
Root mean squared error                 0.7454
Relative absolute error               108.1081 %
Root relative squared error           140.9815 %
Total Number of Instances               9

Correct % = 44.44444444444444
Incorrect % = 55.55555555555556
AUC = 0.5
kappa = 0.0
MAE = 0.5555555555555556
RMSE = 0.7453559924999299
RAE = 108.10810810810813
RRSE = 140.9814753700483
Precision = NaN
Recall = 0.0
fMeasure = NaN
Error Rate = 0.5555555555555556
=== Overall Confusion Matrix ===

 a  b   <-- classified as
 4  0 |  a = yes
 5  0 |  b = no

BUILD SUCCESSFUL (total time: 0 seconds)
```

Our model was built successfully. Once the model was built, we printed the entire results, and then we individually printed the results and the confusion matrix. This is how a model is built with semi-supervised data.

Summary

In this chapter, you learned how to train a model and how to evaluate a clustering model. Then, we looked at the concept of semi-supervised learning, and how it's different from unsupervised learning. Our semi-supervised model has been trained, and we can now make predictions based on it.

Since this was the last chapter of our book, we'll summarize what we have accomplished. You have learned the basics of machine learning; we've installed JDK, JRE, and NetBeans. We looked at search algorithms, working on and implementing two of them: one was Dijkstra's algorithm and the other one was a modification of it (the A* algorithm).

You learned about game playing, and we implemented a game playing algorithm using tic-tac-toe. We covered what a rule-based system is, and we implemented a basic rule-based system in Prolog; then, we used that rule-based system in our Java program. We installed Weka and worked with datasets. We converted a CSV file into an ARFF file, and vice versa. Then, we applied different kinds of filters (supervised and unsupervised filters) to our datasets. We applied very developed classification models. We evaluated, saved, loaded, and made predictions on those models. We did the same with clustering models; we trained our clustering models, and we performed evaluations on our clustering models. Then, you learned the basics of semi-supervised learning, including how to work with semi-supervised learning models.

That's all for this book. Thank you.

Other Books You May Enjoy

If you enjoyed this book, you may be interested in these other books by Packt:

Java Deep Learning Projects
Md. Rezaul Karim

ISBN: 978-1-78899-745-4

- Master deep learning and neural network architectures
- Build real-life applications covering image classification, object detection, online trading, transfer learning, and multimedia analytics using DL4J and open-source APIs
- Train ML agents to learn from data using deep reinforcement learning
- Use factorization machines for advanced movie recommendations
- Train DL models on distributed GPUs for faster deep learning with Spark and DL4J
- Ease your learning experience through 69 FAQs

Artificial Intelligence for Big Data
Anand Deshpande, Manish Kumar

ISBN: 978-1-78847-217-3

- Manage Artificial Intelligence techniques for big data with Java
- Build smart systems to analyze data for enhanced customer experience
- Learn to use Artificial Intelligence frameworks for big data
- Understand complex problems with algorithms and Neuro-Fuzzy systems
- Design stratagems to leverage data using Machine Learning process
- Apply Deep Learning techniques to prepare data for modeling
- Construct models that learn from data using open source tools
- Analyze big data problems using scalable Machine Learning algorithms

Leave a review - let other readers know what you think

Please share your thoughts on this book with others by leaving a review on the site that you bought it from. If you purchased the book from Amazon, please leave us an honest review on this book's Amazon page. This is vital so that other potential readers can see and use your unbiased opinion to make purchasing decisions, we can understand what our customers think about our products, and our authors can see your feedback on the title that they have worked with Packt to create. It will only take a few minutes of your time, but is valuable to other potential customers, our authors, and Packt. Thank you!

Index

54428526R00083